The Blank Page

Iván Argüelles

Several of these poems appeared in the online journal *Caliban*.

© 2021 by Iván Argüelles

All Rights Reserved.

Set in Janson Text with LaTeX.

ISBN: 978-1-952386-08-4 (paperback)
Library of Congress Control Number: 2021942450

Sagging Meniscus Press
Montclair, New Jersey
saggingmeniscus.com

Forsan et haec olim meminisse iuvabit

For Joe and Max

Contents

THE BLANK PAGE	1
BREATHLESS *(THE BLANK PAGE (d))*	5
THE BLANK PAGE	7
THE SYBIL OF CUMAE	8
EMPTYING THE BLANK PAGE	9
THE LAST WORLD WAR	10
THE UNHEARD NOTE	11
THE APOTHEOSIS OF MEMORY	12
SLIP SLIDING AWAY	13
THE UNCOVERED TEXT	14
COME HITHER TO THE AID OF THE PIOUS MORTAL	15
ANOTHER BLANK PAGE	17
WHEN LEAST EXPECTED MAX APPEARED ONE NOON	18
TO VALUM VOTAN	19
DEATH-WATCH	21
ODE TO GINGER PLANT	22
CONSIDERING THE DISTANCES	23
CRANIOTOMY : CHAOS	24
THE SONOROUS CADAVER	25
THE TUMULTUOUS SILENCE	27
EURYDICE'S ECHO	28
SOME STANZAS FOR MAX TWO YEARS AFTER HIS DEATH	29
COMMEMORATING THE INEVITABLE	31
NOT FADE AWAY	32
AN ACCOUNT OF THE RAZING OF THE *TEMPLE*	33
AT THE TOMB OF MEMORY	34
FOSSILS OF LIGHT	35
CUORE MATTO	36

AN AFTERNOON ON MOUNT PARNASSUS	38
YET HAVE THOU PITY AT LEAST ON THE REST ...	39
AND HE FELL FROM HIS CAR ...	40
NELLA SELVA OSCURA	41
A SMALL LOTUS SUTRA	42
A COURSE IN CLASSICAL PHILOLOGY	43
THE ORIGINS OF POETRY IN SOUND	45
ADOLESCENCE	46
PROLEGOMENON TO THE SCOURGE	47
ECHOES	48
THESE DAYS	49
AFTER ALL THIS TIME	50
THE WORLD AS IT IS	51
THE ARCHAIC MOMENT	52
OLVIDOS DE MI PADRE	53
A ROADSIDE EPITAPH	55
GIORNATA DELLA POESIA	56
TULIPS	57
ON THE DEATH OF *VALUM VOTAN* 9 YEARS ON	58
THE POEM I CEASED WRITING	60
TOBOGGAN	61
LA FIN DU MONDE : CHANSON	62
THE GRAMMATICAL ERROR	63
THE NEVER-ENDING SONG	64
COMP LIT I	65
POETRY : A CONFESSION	66
THE RUINS OF PHILOLOGY	67
WHAT IS LITERATURE ?	69
DIANA'S HORN-CALL	70
THE FALCON : A BALLAD	71
HEALED!	72
THE DISCORDANT LYRE	73
AN ODE IN THE TIME OF PLAGUE	74
THE TROUBADOUR'S LAMENT	76
SLEEP , ALL ELSE IS OBLIVION	77
THE APOCALYPSE TODAY	78
IN FAR OFF PROVENCE	79

MEIN JUNGES LEBEN HAT EIN END	80
POMP AND CIRCUMSTANCE BLUES	81
ONE DAY LESS	82
SCHOOL-DAYS : A BALLAD	84
SURVIVING THE DEAD	85
IN PRAISE OF NOTHING	86
THE VOYAGE WITH *CHARON*	87
THE THRONE OF THE GODS	89
APRIL THE CRUELEST MONTH	90
THE ORACLE	91
MEDITATION	92
OMBRE D'INFERNO	94
A GLIMPSE OF THE GODDESS	95
"THE BROKEN HARBOR OF THE SUN"	96
INCUNABULA	97
DARK: THE SUBJECT OF POETRY	98
CRICKET SONG	99
THE CORRUPTION OF LIGHT	100
IVAN AND JOE CREATING GALACTIC CITIES...	102
"SPARKLE"	103
APRIL 20 TWENTY-TWENTY	104
CLASSICAL PHILOLOGY	105
HOW IT STANDS TODAY	107
MESSAGE IN A BOTTLE	108
MISSA BREVIS	109
[FROM *THE HYMN TO GAIA*]	110
"... WITH FACES IN THE DUST"	111
THE SEER IN HIS CUPS	112
SATURDAY MORNING ON THE LIBRARY STEPS	113
HYMN TO THE MUSES	114
THE WORK OF POETRY	115
DANDELIONS	116
SCHOOL-BOY	117
THE SEPULCHER OF MEMORY	118
NIBBANA	119
MNEMOSYNE	120
THREE STANZAS ON AN EPIPHANY	121

IN LOVE WITH LOVE	123
DIDO & AENEAS	125
LACHRYMAE RERUM	126
THE CREATIVE WRITING CLASS	127
THE TOMB OF LIGHT	128
IN THE MERRY MONTH OF MAY	129
THE DAY YOU WOKE FROM A DREAM OF SHADOWS	130
PROGNOSIS : ZERO	132
THE FALL OF TROY	133
AFTER DAYS OF INANITION AND TRANCE	134
MUSING ON ONE'S BRIEF MORTALITY	135
THE AUTOMATIC STONE	136
END-GAME	138
ECHOES ONLY ECHOES	139
THE TIME OF OUR LIVES !	140
AENEAS	141
THE LAUGHING BOY	143
THE GRASS-CUTTER	144
THE HEAD OF *AVALOKITEŚVARA*	146
FOOTNOTE TO LOTUS SUTRA	147
DIDONE ABBANDONATA	148
PHONETIC DECAY	149
THE SHORE IS BRIGHT WITH FLAMES	150
LONG DIVISION	151
DAWN ELEGY	152
KYRIE ELEISON	154
ON A BRIGHT MORNING IN MAY	154
THE HYMN TO *PERSEPHONE*	156
ETERNITY RECONSIDERED	157
THE COCKTAIL PARTY	158
THE ANTIQUITIES !	160
WHITE-ARMED HELEN	161
ADOLESCENCE	162
DREAM SPELL I.	163
DREAM SPELL II.	164
PRIAM	165
THE SIBYL'S MOUTH	166

GNOMIC VERSE	168
TO UNDERSTAND POETRY	169
MEMORIAL DAY 2020	170
THE ROAD NOT TAKEN	171
GOING STEADY	172
AT THE COURT OF AUGUSTUS	173
AD FAUCES GRAVE OLENTIS AVERNI	175
AULA MAGNA	176
CORONA VIRUS SUTRA	177
THE HIGH HOLY DAYS	178
THE BERLITZ METHOD	181
VESTIGES OF A SOLITARY MIND	182
PENTIMENTO	183
KYRIE ELEISON	185
I AM *ORESTES*	186
CIRCE DAUGHTER OF THE SUN	187
TROY	188
THE PHANTOM *HELEN*	189
THE RIDDLE	190
WHAT COMES AFTER OMEGA?	192
NOSTALGIA	193
THE WEIGHT OF MEMORY	194
TEOCALLI	196
THE GARDEN OF PROSERPINA	197
FOOTNOTE TO ILIAD IV, 52	198
LITTLE DEUCE COUPE	200
VENUS IN THE PANDEMIC	201
FEAR OF FALLING	202
IPHIGENIA	203
PARVATI	204
canción del parque Chapultepec	205
LOST IN TRANSLATION	206
THE DEPTHS	207
AFTER SCHOOL	208
ODE : FATHER'S DAY 2020	209
SOME VIRGILIAN STROPHES	210
MIASMA	212

PHILOSOPHY 2020	213
THE ELUSIVE MOMENT	214
FOOTNOTE TO THE MAHABHARATA	215
ALL OF US	216
PIRATE AND TRAVELER	217
DARK AS IT EVER WAS	218
ποίησις	219
IN THE CAVE OF POLYPHEMUS	220
MORTAL ALL TOO MORTAL	222
TROBAR CLUS	223
ELEGY : CORONA VIRUS SUMMER	224
POEMA HUMANO	225
THE FOURTH OF NEVER	226
IMAGE OF JOE PLAYING THE TUBA	227
THE WORLD THIS UNCOMMON PLACE	228
"YET BUT FOR A SCANT SPACE…"	229
VARIATION ON A VERSE OF CAVALCANTI	230
AGAINST THIS MAN WILL I MYSELF ARM ME	230
THE PHOTOGRAPH SHOWING US BROODING	232
THE UNFINISHED NUMBER	233
LE POÈTE MAUDIT	234
APPEARED TO ME A FIGURE OF DEATH	235
I HAVE FOUND A BOOK	236
ONCE UPON A TIME	237
LET NOT AFFECTION FOR THE POET PASS …	238
THE UNFINISHED DESIGN	239
75,600 NEW CASES BREAKING RECORD	240
EPITAPH FROM THE GREEK ANTHOLOGY	241
TOMBSTONE ON VIA APPIA	242
THE UNFINISHED PHOTOGRAPH	243
OFFICE OF THE DEAD	244
DANCING IN THE DARK	245
THE INFERNAL ROUND	246
EJERCICIOS ESPIRITUALES	247

THE BLANK PAGE

THE BLANK PAGE

(a)

the liquid rock
what holds up the fragments
and sequined bolts that flash
the sky as it separates from itself
other scenes blank and borrowed
from sleep a language that dissolves
no sooner is it pronounced
the molten ear !
prosody of grass and gravel
sections of air so tight and wound
around the simplest vowel
a nation of consonants
isolated from syntax
a burden for the mind
to bear a dislocation
symbol of parataxis and depth
either insomnia or fiction
laid out on landscapes
lacking color or sound
the very echo of unconsciousness
lapse from dichotomy and despair
the liquid rock repeated
in the heavens that exist above
the former sky
a canopy of light no broader
than a thumbnail
no more visible than an atom
the loudest sphere of memory
turning on its unseen wheel
a saurian disregard for technology
a mysterious body of water
dark and fathomless
lifted by levers into the third gyre
where Beatrice and Laura
whisper fading words
that none will ever hear
will space ever be re-created ?
jargon of sand drill and leaf
full stop at the chasm
mountain of turmoil

heaving epic written in dust
spear and short-sword cut
across generations
leaving signatures of blood
crimson snakes trailing
in the winds
a theater of living parts
silk is equal to courtesan
in a discourse of curtains
less audible the hair piece
or perfumes that waft
into the pillows
where philology is invented
and statues just born
waking to headless marble
and silent cries of agony
borne by Dawn's small lamp
into the crevice of days
orient and occident split
by the archaic verb *to be*
liquid distances of rock
hematite and beryl
impossible Aztec accents
stone letters on the brow
of a dusky deity
who annihilates the seas
even as the rains commence
their tiny eternities
cigarettes and awnings
paraphernalia of youth
obsolescent and faint
the paling ego
missing evidence
of the negated self
the who I am
of midnight speech

02-04-20

(b)

of midnight speech unraveled
words out of order misplaced
sounds vowels in their distance
of echo and tympanum
the loudest is the symbol
for rho and the least of youths
leaves and twigs snapped
underfoot thud and turf
of memory dim and dusky gone
what brings age on
what withers in mid-air
where black sun and its homophone
vie for light the intransigent
of vision and the yield
of years to dumb fodder
blank pages yearning
turn uselessly in the hills
where meaning diminishes
in mulch and nothing comes back
equestrian statues of high noon
send signals to the planets
a fading is the need and
greening spears miss their mark
how comes the littlest of
the consonants to bear
such weight the insolent
fatigue of speech on the border
of dust and clouds of ire
the gods in their polyphony
who bring doom and backstairs
to smoke and longing
to sleep in arms formless
as billowing waves
that collide senselessly
with childhood's lost fix
pallid pictograms on a sarcophagus
left to float in an azure tide
with sulfur phantoms
revolving in the broken kaleidoscope
of history the self that
burns the mask that recites

the unwritten text
while the great *Autocrat Time*
in a single swerve
removes all of us from
the unbearable mirror
of make-believe

02-06-20

(c)

> "Lo, *a man accepteth recompense from
> the slayer of his brother, or for his dead son*"
> *Iliad IX, 632-633*

I'm not going to go through that again
sent by Hera owl-eyed Athena visible only
to Achilles you know the rest dominant
accent tonic shining through vowels
curtailed by time and put his short-sword
back into the sheathe and waited for mother
Thetis to pray if only the seas the raucous
waves and sleep diminished by a thought
mortality on the ridge of stars greening in
memory's adolescent binge and telling
someone in the ear's shot echo about
place names and situations that perhaps
never and the fuming et cetera standing
outside the coke bottle and cigarette held
famously nonchalant for the girls behind
their curtain of impermanence so would
today only be an asterisk in limbo a version
of forewarned grass and the brief light
of a sun already blackened behind the eye
cyclopean astigmatism of history the guess
that tomorrow may not be a conscious decision
you and I brother the singers not the song
who will remember by the grieving shore
which was which Agamemnon glaring into
the glassy antipodes and the Greek as ever
one step from comprehension stars studding
the garrulous but opaque western heights

which we assumed was for all time an approach
outside of literature as put to us in classes
occidental definitions of essay and rhymed
patterns set to myth an arm or a shoulder
dolorous in their organization and night
too omnipresent and without etymology
the exact and razor-sharp cut in the temple
offerings of fattened thighs incense and rite
and yet to be at a loss totally enigmatic
turning the corner to find one's self alone
where did they all go the outlined recall
of denim fitted heroes brawling bright
and ignorant of their futility

02-07-20

BREATHLESS (THE BLANK PAGE (d))

red the squiggle the space of death
all spots brighter than the blackest sun
in one place or nowhere at all without
beginning and never stops the thought
speed of mind untraced the unending
design borderless the fluid enormity
serpentine the primitive water below
and four hundred and twenty skies above
each a metal of stone artifact of ether
aerial masses too bright to interpret aright
and memory itself half-way up the stairs
with nowhere else to fall but to the left
where directions give birth to distance and
distances embroider the birth of the gods
thirty three thousand trillion of them
disposable as light-particles in a cyclotron
sound itself the brief echo in a wavelength
of eternity wrapped around a swirling axle
upon which pivots the molten chariot
of unrecorded history the chronos and
division of time into infinite hemispheres
each smaller than its mirrored opposite
or failing to take this into account metaphor
and spiral swerve and dereliction cycle
and homophone the longing to be *other*

in a fractured kaleidoscope of previous
universes the instant of becoming *nothing*
+ +
were we ? grasshoppers by day
lightning-bugs by night were we ?
we saw the nation of fire in the eye of grass
we saw the next day of creation annihilated
in the pebble we skipped across the riverbed
suns at least a trillion of them passed into
the nameless hills that marked day's eternal end
and if we slept it was in the grain of sand
that contains all of space and what lies outside
we learned math from the willow leaf torn
from its excited and mourning voice root
of all desires in the moment of final dying
death and its triplicate followed us in and out
of the ziggurat of grammar and nonsense
it was all a dream within a dream that we
ever were twins in a pyramid of echoes
distances yearning to be even more remote
the triangle and the dust-heap mosaic
that the eye ravels and unravels daily as
long as breath worked its bellows inside
the map of the cosmic oven and we burned
as in Vedic hymns to *Agni* twin of *Indra* !
+ +
breathless the comet returns its tail
to the grieving shape of gravity
new stars older already than the first
aspire to perception and dissipate
their fiery energy in a single whoosh
out of sight never heard totally unknown
the origin of the end before it starts
Brother ! in which inch of heat do you
keep appearing and disappearing ?
summers in the molten glass of illusion
next to you I lay my head of stone
unconscious passion of the invisible

02-08-20

THE BLANK PAGE

(e)

slashed at either end
the volume of air its literal
and symbolic parts its fictions
of syntax and order the deictic
particles all colored red
and memory the victim
of its own sleep becoming distance
unalterable and infinite
why go on—it was so sweet
and skipping from joy to joy
immersed in the day's briefest
light the adorable one on a chariot
golden wheeled spinning in
the happy moment of transcendence
can a single calligraphic deviation
cause so much grief ? when ?
to go back to the time before time
the spindle of gasses roaring
silently in the foreboding ear
the chisel of flame the imminence
of the ethereal cliff downsized
by the velocities of heat and longing
did the cosmos supersede itself ?
what are accidents of oil and surf ?
the Eye ! seeing what it can
and wants to the visible *Whole*
coming apart in the instant
of realization and passion
is sound itself a misrepresentation ?
all the words imaginable cannot
substitute for the manifest world
shoulder and hip and brow
come into relief and are blessed
by as many gods as it takes to die
here is the number one and across
the street the other number one
and the pain of becoming two
and soon the highway disappears !
which of the many blades of grass
is the eternal one ?

who can explain ? darkness is great
it comes repeatedly to take us
into its senseless embrace
even as we tie our shoes
oblivion which is never far
and the smallest rain
and night unending

02-09-20

THE SYBIL OF CUMAE

mortal all too mortal the shoulder
followed by a trip to the arm and wrist
not to speak of the knee in its broken cathedral
mornings dawn in disarray of darkness
punctuated by windows of tainted starbright
threats to moor the boat before noon
to empty the canvas of its tinctures of iodine
and ravel the silk skein one last twist
around the dozen unpronounceable words
used to ward off death and its scavengers
and memory and the littered epistles
of thought evocations of lost topographies
a city underneath another city where vacated
tenements still house remnants of personae
weary the waking eye the fossil cognition
the sudden realizations of the limit
to the calendar of days pockmarked cicatrix
juxtapositioned realms of dusk and gloaming
is it the back-door the hand must approach ?
Shiva or his likeness last seen crouching
on the stoop waiting to proclaim the *Mountain* !
vagaries of eurocentric myth the world
without a script stage blackened by calumny
and political rhetoric the mirror turned inside
out to avert phantoms who mourn their
lack of light and the mangle of Latin distichs
excavated in an Etruscan dumping ground
what is earth but a sand-trap and midden heap
pot-shards and incunabula for fireflies
horizons the color of ants and heaven
no larger than a thimble full of lye and salt

where is there to return ? in what opaque
mire of mind does a paradise exist a shine
a raiment however rent that white was
and shoes that fit someone else's feet
and the grandeur of a lawn separated from
the porch by eons of adolescent raving
the moon ! the sun and its vitreous homophone !
pyramids that walked through history stone
and rubble and empyrean of pre-cosmic
disorder the volume of sound turned up
deaf ! what will the doctor prescribe today ?
the minute's up the water-clock's run dry
a scribble of errant syllables the Sybil's cant
and visceral the fear that what she has to say
this time is meant for you alone !

02-10-20

EMPTYING THE BLANK PAGE

comparing the sounds of the world's ruins
the vowels and attributes of breath and
depths resonating beneath the broken bone
the oval and the fix and the melancholy
poetry breeds at the nexus of cloud and angel
the incomplete travels of light through sleep
convulsive rock formations grassy steeps
devotion to the blue-faced god and to the
golden one in whose lap *all* beings settle forever
so it goes in the faulty zone where memory
wavers on the middle step and the clauses
about smoke and catastrophe about sirens
that bring on black noons and the vibrating
suns circling the consonants that compose
thought and matter breviary and testament
of grief the afternoon after the blaze and ash
the furious instant when the page empties
of all its corollaries and silvery ghosts provoke
words to proceed meaninglessly from the oracle
listening for mortal reckoning in the knuckle-bone
the wee hour when the dusky steeds set forth
bearing phantom universes in their foamy wake
afar ! look the haze and crown of human fate

each has a single shirt or a handle that does not fit
there are hours in the sanitarium with rumors
that dress distances like women in mourning
and the apse where lamps flicker transcending
their own vocabulary and to wake disconsolate
hearing the gods bicker over the ignition and
what brings down the cosmos aflutter in leaves
hard by the dry well and the children come
to slake their thirst already dead in their joy
flakes of light samples of sky seraphic notes
tubular instances of recognition before dark

02-11-20

THE LAST WORLD WAR

the meadow asleep long into the dark
the people who remember are all gone
the iota and its flint the tender absence
flickering disregards for the world's toil
ancient rock that precedes eternal death
perched on the edge that divides light
from space and the syllables culminating
in the oracle's lack of clarity a loudness
none can hear the frozen intaglio of mind
much as thought can bear before dissolving
verses discontinuous scattered in the grass
like fingers looking for missing number three
which is the amount it takes to bring twilight
across the last horizon where mountains
are but a mythographer's dusky conjecture
it is at odds with itself the cavernous length
extended across the origins of space right
where clouds are born in seraphic raiment
the fossil sky ! dust of light and figures big
as the halos around the newly risen sun
black orb of the heavens increasing hemispheres
between north and the endless south of the dead
how long will it keep lying there in serpentine
disguise of night even as day forms its vowels
sounding the filmy ends of time in a fugue of
impossibilities that drill the ear like honey
spirals of pollen and leaves chattering Vedic

where are gone the many and refulgent gods
of distance and silk ? from peak to peak fire
dances feminine and shifting enormous hair
incandescent as the full moon in its ocean
far below puny warriors of the Mahabharata
clangor and pitch of elephant and chariot
raise purposeless ash of illusion to the skies
drift deep into the last breath of the cosmos
planet after planet extinguished punctuation
haunted evenings of an insect afterworld
it is to this end we once played in the light

02-12-20

THE UNHEARD NOTE

the vowels long and short
thirty three hymns to them alone
winds and torrents of air and skies
broken in halves and the numinous bright
sundered in meaning *sound* alone remains !
who determines the next flight out ?
which of the multiple and tumultuous deaths
is ascribed to the sacred and unknown syllable ?
Poet ! vatic nonsense ! unravel the skein of air
turbans and hooves and the weight of trees
sections of light too heavy to bear in life
the ancient paths where have they gone ?
the fundament and the depths of darkness
out of which shining the marvelous deities
arise for a moment only all eye and spleen
whence the doctrine of illusion and birth ?
who and how many and wherefore all moving
shaking in the limitless inch of time are they ?
you were here once and I alongside playing
the tune on roads of watered brick and dust
you disappeared ! a haven of dew and sparkle
wherever the sight swerved tracks of cinder
tiny prints like those of holy deer
archaic with longing to understand the speech
of cloud and lightning and brief afternoons
who can count the consonants the numberless
are there no hymns chanted for them ?

the names for all the spaces in between words
how are they pronounced and why in all this grief ?
numb and hallowed the foot-steps up and down
the unmarked stairwell and then where ?
you were a shadow a fancy prince a sapling
when the small catastrophe struck in the cheek
today as on no other the various and silent hymns
dedicated to all the noises in the universe
resound with all the capacity of stone
nothing comes back no echo no hue of tone
only the unvariable sweep of the Chasm
swirling inside the endless unheard *Note*

02-12-20

THE APOTHEOSIS OF MEMORY

wind-chimes of Versailles !
illustrious composers in search of velocity
unseen agent of stage and screen
dressed as a shaking leaf and the crown of desire
the tell-tale signature of the winds
offspring of Rudra who blot out the eye of the sun
what is natural discourse if not consumption
of energy to the point of dissolution
blanched filigrees of memory the very dust
of light and the egress of matter
through the narrow siphon of sleep
ages to resound in the small rock left
pivoted near the entrance to the sky
and of the waters rushing through the pupil
of the deified Herakles and the pinnacle of fury
feminine in shape and speed in the star-map
where the ghost of *Mnemosyne* steps
with her phantom embroideries of distance
and the delicate vowels that surround her
all wanting to be returned to their former selves
shape and orient the ornament of mortality
carved from a single blade of grass her stairway !
oracles in decibels of high zero and the alpha
of all enumerations in their planetary dress
and what of *Rodasi* goddess of the two worlds ?
shining and not shining the space between them

the revolving door of perpetuity and fame
the success of a mirror ! everything disappears
dew and ash and even the eternal flame
space was an accident of ignition
sundered from the chronologies of air
devastated as well by the plenitude of light
bright ! thunder of the invisible hemispheres
drawn ever upwards into the annuities of immortality
only to be forever forgotten come the crash
the insubordinate rule of the *circularities*
heat and diapason fountains of breath
Memory ! exhaled against the vitreous fragment
etched by a finger of fog and erased
who will ever be the last to remember *her*
figment of the dance of time ?

02-13-20

SLIP SLIDING AWAY

no sooner does the wind change shape
then the world devolves to its nickel size
and the shouts of oblivion and glee the kids
in the playground at the end of the day
when the *Stranger* comes to take his share
and sun already a distance of hills and vowels
obscurities and demands of smaller hands
the briefness imparted to tousled hair the
articulation of a simple note played on a comb
the intransigence of the color red at the window
beckoning for a fast emulation of glass
how great the chaos of unlimited Jupiter
like the basements of failed department stores
so everything just collapses in the minute
of transfiguration toys and mottled rags
afternoons lived on the tip of a spear
the battle ! wholesale carnage of ripe fruit
devils tiny and grinning inside their wounds
streets named after the absences of the week
months rolled into a single bandaged finger
grass and leaf and the entire panoply of stars
who will care for the one the *Stranger* touched ?
to accept as fate the unnumbered diseases

the transfusions and fever-blisters and
to reckon the thermometer's empyrean
is it heat ? do the gods employ ether ?
who was the last to turn off the light ?
implore the knees not to buckle so swiftly !
it must be vengeance of white-armed Hera
devastating the checker-board folly of Troy
one cliff after another falls like sand mounds
in the playground where rust assumes command
swings lilting slightly in the empty rain
and no one to pick up the shadows left behind
you can hear the crying in the ampersands
the ditto of a pen trying to recall a signature
din and roar of the unpronounceable syllable
why is grief the chiefest emotion on the radio
where a turn-style revolves endlessly in the dark
what is new is the latest death wrapped
in aluminum foil and the nicks and cuts
and to watch the intricacies of a life ebb
and the *Stranger* in the corner sobbing
and the *Stranger* in the corner weeping
slip sliding away murmurs a whisper
slip sliding away

02-14-20

THE UNCOVERED TEXT

as winter's mourning comes to close
the skins of water that disguise the sky
drift sleepily across the western hills
bird and serpent and quoits of fiery drizzle
the world's natural face returns to dark
who preceded us in the enigmatic trek
across the untrammeled inch of space
across the unspoken vow to be as ever free
arms akimbo and eyes averted from the call
whose depths none can ken and clouds
iridescent silent that enter the eye unawares
a tear in the fabric of distance a torn leaf
convulsed vowels yearning to form a sound
literature of diapason and solitude writ
small at the bottom of the blankest page

the diary of a *Siren* in her aphasia
winds whose architecture of invisibility
falls apart at the merest mention of glass
the child in the man ! the woman foremost !
clepsydras and metronomes that divide
the human soul from its prismatic frame
abounding in memory the small hand
reaches out across the totem sketch of time
trying to recover the imagination of its fingers
but for the sighs of nurses in the House-of-Death
down under or even as far off as Mount Meru
slate gray seasons pass through a fingernail
Vishnu ! wherever azure is a juggernaut
the wheel that rolls in defiance of gravity
upwards to the molded doors of ether
behind which thirty three deities of smoke
conspire to reveal the phonetic ladder
texts of hieratic inspiration diaspora of *Light !*
or is it a demon unrolling the palm-leaf script
raveled detonations of silence !
still we are left puzzled in the tomorrow
known only to rock fragments and grass
listening but not knowing why for the echo
of a tiny flute with three trembling notes
the uncovered text the riddle of the stars
it is either shining or it is not shining

02-15-20

"COME HITHER TO THE AID OF THE PIOUS MORTAL"
Rg Veda, vii, 71.2

the riff in the orient twelve days long
sufficient to ignore how little time remains
a mortal existence hanging on a thread of air
colorless and vapid the extension of thought
hopelessly entangled in the dubious clouds
emerging from the hidden socket in the blue
high ! flight on the wings of sleep over hill
and dale the syllabic entries of an oracle
miscomprehension and rock at the one end

and at the other mankind's wavering portal
to success and salvation a cracked mirror
at best a softened cushion for the headache
the sliver of moon inserted in the eye-piece
who will ever understand these adumbrations
forced to accept a sharpened shaft in the heart
like the abc's of a lunar session on teratology
the beast ! demons as beautiful and hallucinating
as they are destructive with their cancers and
face-lifts the approximation to the Muse
formfitting stocking over the head and dactylic
lilies surfacing on the alligator skin of memory
how does anything happen once it's over ?
magma and oblivion you look all around you
wondering how the battle ever got this far
the unwieldy chariot the reins loosened the horses
turned to instant flame lacerated atmospheres
which are the stuff of history texts scribbled
in paragraphs of aphasia and amnesia mimosas
looking for the sun to touch once before blackening
and bouquets of thought delivered to the door-step
where riddled with vices a deity sits smoking calm
and indifferent to the clash of oxygen and nitrous
sit up ! wake to the beauties of hummingbird and
asp the crawling sands the livid bruises of cliffs
seas rising to walk on stilts of boric acid
mountain crashing on mountain and the jazz
of unlimited sound captured inside a metal disc
the apocalypse ! children ! ambulances ! love !
world is a perpetual motion machine gone awry
window on eternity second traffic light to the left
let me off ! hamadryads in see-through skin
a warning that their woods are disappearing
beyond that it is impossible to say a fortnight
may be all that remains to the allotted chaos
rivers shining in their bright night convulsed
with the voices of leaves torn and rattling
into the star-brittle darkness a lapse and a fume
little smidgeons of flickering edges of ancient
and what is left of the peninsula and its vowel
a stuttering godhead a vague incoherent sound
how does anything happen once it's over ?

02-16-20

ANOTHER BLANK PAGE

pilgrimage to the Holy Land !
with no ink and no bottle
wave follows wave of gold
sun at last has put down
its blackened sheets to sleep !
a saddle and a Hispanic lexicon
horses of pure dust and camp
blazes argent fringed fists
canned moonlight spelling
an end to literature
vernacular vowels only !
a headless statue proclaims
that noon is eternity
all other hours mere blanks
in the unending paragraph
of space the incorruptible
and for every consonant
in the variety of echoes
there is a beginning to
but not the end of a poem
it is a woman and only !
she is a postcard ampersand
a stunning virtue of wrists
the water of a river that
runs underneath the ocean
which reflects and does not
reflect the shining of mind
she is the literal nothing !
it is nine o'clock in bedlam
it is nowhere on the road
to the Sanctuary of birds
the holy and the profligate
lain by the ditch the corpse
talking and wheedling
the discourse on the Syllable
between monster and fraud
sulfur tongues bruiting aloud
the harrowing of the Void !
finally there is hair by the mile
lengths and skeins of silky
black reticulation the Universe !

and when that is not enough
death-pale lip gloss and
eyelashes that weigh a ton
mountains shorn of wings
where sacred weddings hold
Cadmus and Harmony
freight loads of opium
banners depicting the boar
in golden crescent and hands
that have lost their shape
moving in reveries across mists
everything is in blank verse
suggestions of infinity
more suggestions of infinity !
it is a woman and only !

02-16-20

WHEN LEAST EXPECTED
MAX APPEARED ONE NOON

Max you come at me
like an explosion of fireflies
though it is broad daylight !

every day in the hospital
was an eternity but the last day
was the briefest infinity on record
the coming and going of existence
molecules painted red and black
fever charts and small diapasons
of breathing and entire dimensions
of space inverted inside an eyelid
which direction were you going
when the detonation of silence
occurred ?

small winds in the leaves smaller
yet the air embroidered with sunlight
a finger an eyelash the immensity !
everything for an instant fused
with gravity and a pounding
in the ear and the swirling of

all the colors in a thumbnail
up and down all gone
finished the length of corridor
the fluorescent rug
footfalls in the mulch
disquieting size of metal
vibrating somewhere
in the back of time

there must have been angels
watching beings we imagine
out of grief to justify the event
seraphic faces of pure distance
memory itself and nothing more
watching when you exited
from the fevered shell
innocently unkempt
days exist no more
only screens that separate
space from time and swarms
of fireflies exploding like noon
of all the hours the emptiest
and the shadow of light
falling on blind statues
and the echo of words
that will never be
understood

02-18-20

TO VALUM VOTAN

*"Reading book after book the whole world died,
and none ever became learned!"*

Kabir

how is it in following the course of the sun
you missed a step fell backwards into the well
black night enveloped you even as you donned
that bright cloth and set forth while retreating
into the unknown Word and absolved of all
principle entered unawares the mansion of *Yama*
when you called out in the hoarse whisper

familiar to rock fragments and grass clumps
I could no longer hear what you meant by
so many unassorted syllables the heights perhaps
the roaming hills the rivers spilling out of
the brows of the mountains that hovered like
clouds over the perpetual summer we shared
in the long ago beside the shadow of the *other*
watching attentively our every movement and
the chasms that occurred in the crease of time
the years of four hundred days ! magnificent
cities coiled around a shining like serpents
and the mouthing of incantations and numerals
incomprehensible unless you were unaware in
a drug-trance floating from rooftop to rooftop
the radiance of an instant borrowed from eternity
come down , Joe ! naked bathed in the saliva
of a demoness whose multiple embraces and
perfumed smoke and pierced temples stunned
quickening the breath for a lifetime you thought
it wasn't so and there were threads crimson and
gold like hieroglyphs scattered across a water
lifted from the embryo of an unborn day a sun
many suns darkening like bracelets on your arms
swift and cunning shafts feathered and wild
flew into your heart and drunk on mescal or pulque
you became turquoise desert mirage shifting from
altar to altar the loud and the supreme silence
one with the avatars of cactus and basalt a cipher
nine years now engraved into the tumulus of a myth
winding through the cordilleras of our childhood
and still listening for the echo of your words
to come back across the Ocean-of-Being I wait
it is only inches between the living *you* and
the dead *you* in the fierce empty of space
only a step away from the other side of time

02-19-20

DEATH-WATCH

three leagues below the surface
where sleep derives its etymology
and I am looking askance and I am
on the verge of the pit and whatever
night draws from the silence of leaves
speech acts of limb and branch and
without gravity and loosed in the maze
of winches and astral pulleys and ampersands
and the burning waters of the Phlegethon
the camera-man keeps his eye on the bird
to be detonated any minute and who will
make the bed and who will lower the roof
and sleeping like an adolescent angel
as always the lineaments of death
writ sweet and tender on his brow
will it be as predicted a whisper
without sleeves and the embryonic winds
born in the new grass of the western slope
I am a mountain and I transgress all steps
Vishnu! it is speaking in script
low bass tones frictions of light and poppy
the legend of the hair-line the crease
prepared by the Turkish surgeon
and talk talk talk quality of life and
bedside machines to lift and lower
and the toxic rejuvenation of ideas about
the length and duration and the moon
who is circling like an eye sunk deep
in the syntax of mind and rock the heights !
suffice to say air has run out of time
isotope and quanta and freshets rills
clear waters blackening by noon when sun
reaches a zenith of madness and bright
how many hands will it to take to grasp ?
alone I go it says in the depths
on the edge of the abyss and the cries
described by Dante in the pitch
and the body in its magnet and foil
whirling senselessly at a loss for sheets
yellow effluvia of thought on the brink
the passion to omit the omegas

one by one as they approach
three wild strides !
and that is all

02-20-20

ODE TO GINGER PLANT

brow against the wailing wall of psychiatry
flush red ginger hued elemental bass-line
drum throb syncopation up the spine
her ladder of crimson hair and jade-stone
for eyes a pair of lamps green as electricity
riding the "el" round and round a hang over
when to get off and then miss the next train
oiled black metal suns turning cycles of envy
delivery to Long Island in a symmetry of alephs
curtailed doom the busy intersection where
memory turns to a single vowel drugged wrapped
and pronounced AUM if waking is a suggestion
and the filthy dawn streets cramps and sections
of eastern sky air thick as slabs of mortuary
sheets looking for the plate glass that beholds
the first drink of the day could be it and
when she never turned up for the wedding
and lay in upturned bed clothes a waif of wealth
who could analyze her Jungian depths her
anti-desires pub crawling up Third Avenue
around the time of the Kennedys and despair
the iron-maiden inflicted on the American conscience
a world away in the waist deep swamps of Nam
could be her name alone possessed the magic
to dispel an afternoon's glassy ennui a trophy
of bright but ultimately confused not a honey moon
but a backtrack on a dream-camel through sands
gritty as Sinatra's voice three AM or San Juan de la Cruz
waiting in an empty aerodrome and voices piped
through the metal sheathes of antiquity proclaiming
an end to Arcadia and the Mosaic Law
a pocket full of Greek myth and washer women
scrubbing the subway floor and isn't it a shame
button up the wrong way shirt's on backwards
crumpled envelope of defiant poems tossed aside

the flickering gold leaf of Jamaica bay at pre-dawn
when the rutilating horses maddened by the Socratic
gadfly storm the looming clouds that demand
thunder-burst and a hint of the fetid tropics
chattering in a secret Pepper-Rican tongue
solipsism and mercury in a gilded jazz horn
dreamily slurring tidal notes of grief by the Hudson
a barrack of sinister deaths held for a moment
before the class resumes the discussion
of the Aristotelian properties of drama
tottering Orestes and bawling Clytemnestra
and in the back row Ginger Plant eyes covered
a shade of cinnamon shadow her flushed cheeks
writing a small goodbye to Joe . . .

02-21-20

CONSIDERING THE DISTANCES

the rivers the totality of them
and the stars whose enemy are *they* ?
unless a man is spiritual of what worth is he ?
a demon among us a prowling snake
a mortal hungry for what he doesn't know
a phantom who erects over night excuses
to go on breathing and the lustrous contours
of light the all pervading and yet and yet
seated on this stone in the night amidst
the fleet of bad memories of things gone wrong
the spirit becomes void weeping its error
the naked mistaken wood the forlorn path
over stony distances going nowhere
the faces unaddressed at the wrong moment
and *why didn't I hold his hand in the end* ?
asked over and over the plunged mind
unable to assert its own fictions in waters
rising the darkness of it all the game
of pick and choose what a foil !
into whose piteous eyes do we gaze this now
unsure the quadrant of sky veers to the left
angelic stammering in the dimmed relics
of cloud and woof the trammeled sensations
that we have never done enough to ward off

and the sinister entities the feelings
of make believe and the books behind them
and the sutures opening up in mid air
the conscious step taken backwards the heights
enervating injustices of hills that cannot be reached
never asked for this life didn't know why
it was given if it was to be so misgoverned
and this and that of rationale debate to no point
the argument of bright and the suffused thought
that creates its own winter lamp only
to have it extinguished unawares and grief
the gods on their peaks smitten by the gamble
watching the senseless ply of the loom
colors unravel sounds the debacle of echo
the human print erased in the sands
who was ever in control ?

02-22-20

CRANIOTOMY : CHAOS

if order is not observed
and no smoke proceeds from the altars
to no avail the ritual vowels the ministrations
of digit and echo as sky impounds darkness
the balance between distance and the unknown
mere configurations of breath and intaglio
curvature of space diagnosis of disorder
chaos in the unrelenting moment
of total cessation when the visible becomes
the last vestige of memory on the rack
symbols of light and mercury the fast
and bright planets in their embryos racing
to take the great white lunar stone
dissolving it in the compound of absence
and who of the many children running
in the fresh dawn of grass will be first
to lay down the body returning to earth its brief
and puzzled shadow and the sorrowing
from the trees will ascend the vacant sound
the lamenting between leaf and leaf
the small and minute issue of air becoming
ruddy and still and the multiple grief

resounding in the immense rock fragments
the very outskirts of matter vanishing
temple ruin landslide unending silence
+ + + + + + + + + + + + + + + – + + + + + + + + + + + + + + + +
long histories of the forbidden scalpel and
wreck of the hairline and versions of angel
in the ceiling's indistinct anatomy how many
eons back in the second or third cosmic
disasters and the misnomers of hope and
lesions in each blade of grass and the size
of six blood cells magnified for their error
a wood and a meadow and the troubled brook
running through cold systems of ether
and voices the remnants of a tragic *Bang!*
fossil specimens of cloud and their wounds
immensities of the thumb-nail and verb
that conjugated reveals the hand's ancient
shape the archaic latitudes inherent to stone
the oracular ear and its phonetic decay
riddled with secret rumors about heaven
the tiny but intricate space-ship floating
away once and for all from its sad mooring
vast and senseless pointillism of doubt
the mortal moment in its lost code
fragments fading in a maternal echo
dot dot dot

02-23-20

THE SONOROUS CADAVER

I sing distance the dark and everlasting
and whatever preceded that dark and the
eventualities of tone and heights the joy
surrendering the weight to the unseen
measuring the shadow not by what it seems
but by how it disappears and the ominous
and great black sun and the visible
but untouchable deities who have the right
to return to mansions with dustless floors
the heavens they call them and the flowers
strewn over mountains like battlefields
with beautiful corpses I chant and rave

the vedic undercuttings of thought bright
the dawn and her untrammeled horses
ruddy and a-sweat pacing out the number
of days the specious and uncounted nights
the elements that compose memory's body
the chaste and oiled and soon forgotten
members keen on the race glistening in
the foreboding afternoon and twilight
the sudden with its diminished hills and
speech effects the clouds roaming spaces
with remote traces of vowel and echo all
the darknesses that follow the first one
enters and never comes back and music
rising out of the trampled lawn the leaf
torn from its choir of silent voices the one
I used to be and no longer am the flutter
in the air after a ghost has passed and hair
the quickened comb the silhouette of hands
searching but never finding what they
left behind in the tumult of instruments
tuning up in the grotto where philosophers
ruminate on the impending nothingness
where did the gods learn to shine they ask
each blinder than the other fingers of grass
askance the notched string to play a single
reverberating note the singing I listen and
hard by the stone well and the cautious
mind trying to retain something of its cause
the highest sounds are nothing but rock
cut from the abyss of time when it was and
before the sigma and the rho chasing braids
of flame into the utter and then I hear again
the purpose and the fuse the loud and the
simple serenity if only it could be that way
always and forever the darkest loam where
laid to rest the dust it was being *there*

02-24-20

THE TUMULTUOUS SILENCE

who supports the page of air the still
leaf shifting in its dark molded sleep
the fist of a divinity like glass in water
shapes its unseen shadow in defiant law
and yet the sounds of words unheard
echo in the split blade of grass and sky
looms like a mirror of halves that none
can discern but by the black sun's eerie
lamp the pedestal of graven stone earth
and its portents of disyllabic death a spear
sustained by gravity piercing the heart
like fires at the end of time the instant
of shattering visible and invisible of
the encumbered ego on its mirage of horses
who inflates this wind of errors raging
though its *selva oscura* and notches peaks
with vowels both long and short a grammar
of impossibilities in the brief afternoon
of fragmented rock and solitary song
how memory clings with slipping fingers
to the soft decay of shape and the brow
furrowed in thought of afterwards and
no inkling of the unpaved hour extending
its curtailed path into the great Unknown
we question the passing minute the banner
and the chariot and the small trumpet vine
that resounds in the drinks that stand iced
on the tray who dares to take and down
the shattered infinity of that echoing time
didn't any one notice the missing One
the *other* who arrived too late and spoke
not a whisper and like a telephone attached
to the opposite wall ringing in the clouds
hello to all the deaths that intervene
to the mistakes and jots and blanked out
lines of testament and poetry or goodbye
at last once and for all the famous ending
unnoticed in the reverie and tumult
thunderous remote in the dreaming ear
punctuations erased and papers tossed
aside into the furious ditch of envy and

then ask again who supports the page of air
the transient heavens of a forgotten day
who but the small corpse in his hieroglyph
set sail into the billowing beyond breath

02-25-20

EURYDICE'S ECHO

Eurydice what is it a blank page
but the errors in the path the triangles
and associations of unseen rivers running
a gamut of echoes into the seething waters
in a riot of memories of unsung verses
of issues regarding the right and left
hemispheres of the light that has failed
Eurydice a justice of forms that do not fit
of shoes and sleeves and the *one* only
regarding the dark under the bed silent
and like chrome somehow illicit a weight
less than simple the aggravation of air
gathering like a ball of crimson thread
in the unaccustomed brain the cold hum
of machines meant to keep the body going
Eurydice the plaint of depths unkenned
hand over hand and nothing ! what are
quoits and bees and loud letters beginning
with "A" and the fuel of intensity the head
coming to its own conclusions the vowel
and semaphore turned to a blinking green
can it ever be other than the missed curve
plunging into the mountain and the wings
invisible and moving through punctuation
a zed and a metamorphosis of ampersands
Eurydice herself the small inconstancy of
sound in the absent fist the gorgeous replica
of hair and at last breath coming out of its
sheath becoming and then going away
night wraps its grasses around the symbol
and stars that are the notes of a song
harp and strum and leather indentations
tightening the wrist so the soul can't flee
Eurydice alone the unkempt decibel of voice

and turned back and to dust incremental
and twilight the faint footfalls the hoarse
oracular throat fading fast and gone
Eurydice

02-26-20

SOME STANZAS FOR MAX
TWO YEARS AFTER HIS DEATH

i

sun for what is it other than grass
foot once where trodden the simple
heat in circles wouldn't such a day
had been the smallest detail green
and bright even when darkest the
lamp of eternity his brief face to
one side walking narrow the fleet
folded up into quarters a page now
blank gone fused to narrow switch
feel so absent the rays blackening
around shallow hills the speech of
accident and thought asterisks glow
when even it isn't so no more you
know it doesn't and the distances
only like sorrowing afternoons a
grief the toy it used to play shaking
numbers don't mean nor floors
come to meet the hour's spindle
snapped in spine the two won't
come together meld and sweep
away dust the shadow and shelve
each letter on the back penned
the quivering ink a finger lost

ii

ants blackened by the fierce bewildering
sun jumping from chariot to chariot a wild
sum of names Achilles Arjuna and Aeneas
does one use the word *ten-thousand*
to address the gods then why the weeping
dense and uncontrolled in the thick Dravidian

wood abounding with questions and vines
the tiger embossed on the small mimosa leaf
arisen from the former ocean and all the roads
go south only south carrying the radios
of the dead and the prickly pear cactus and
how can the innumerable ants and the blackest
form of night the man outside the rain and
whiplash and transfusion so much and so little
to remember him by the excrescent foliage
which is the window of sound the Sumerian
vowel-system attuned to the stars and acrylic
and lace and the foam that happens between
planets Venus and Mercury this has to end
the lungs can receive no more and the blasts
from the anvil Oh I am so

iii

and here falls the drama curtain and
word of voices spliced on the revolving
tape of night magnetic and brown hills
as it were resound the ear is full of pitch
and the howls of the trodden grass evening
in the porch and the lamps lit by fireflies
that in turn exaggerate the consonants lined
up and named after extinct stars a blur of
fancy and memory trading ideas about the
size of a circle or directions like east towards
the mountain on sale in the cheap dry-goods
basement coming and going flak of ivory
please using the indirect command and
honorific pronouns hands alone distinguish
how accomplished is the piano and the
least of which is the shadow boxer on the right
half a century old and fists of invisibility
a wonder such beauty still radiates the hair
ever a season without combs a sample reddened
in the bright of a perfervid afternoon in Akkad
who will explain the mysteries of dying

iv

is it dust of course the universe has no
other explanation you come into so-called

being and are possessed by light and learn
the speech of mortals and there are wounds
secrets that invest the soul with ether and
the ampersands of a surgical trial in limbo
if you are awake for the remainder and
someone tugs at your sleeve you are handed
a cane with which to address the statues that
somehow crowd the sidewalks will give
way to you passing it seems a shadow

02-27-20

COMMEMORATING THE INEVITABLE

this is the end of the world's three manifestations
egoless matter ! no birth ! no death !

how often and many strapped into a gurney
taken away in an ambulance to
the deserted mountain retreat of Shiva
does time repeat itself in small ligatures ?
are there bewildered Chinese monks working
to translate the *Lankavatara Sutra* ?
there are blanks centuries long that occur
between yesterday and today and a syntax
composed entirely of grief and honorific pronouns
there are phonemes and punctuations and echoes
lexical entries that have no gravity or height
and leaves each smaller than the other
that commune with the world of thirsty ghosts
and islands of pure distance with syllabic dialects
calling and calling but getting no answer
two years or two days what is the difference
in the abacus of unrecorded history ?
is anything left behind in the dust-storms of memory ?
what continues to pulsate in the empty sleeve ?
is there a voice asking for its rows of buttons or
a hand that speaks no more than an ear can stammer ?
forget the tool that opens doors !
the divinity is replete with aphasia and amnesia !
the tongue ! words ! a crimson splash against rock
eternities in a dew drop and fractions
of light contained in its dark cradle
it was a dream the body ever walked its own trace

come back ! planets rotating within quotation marks
devastations of air and diseases forever undetected
toys and arithmetic and cloudy afternoons
fusion of metal to music and silence
the loudest the inarticulate and most beautiful
vanishing in the bamboo grove growing
unbeknownst on the other side of the mountain
come back ! *I am here*
                    (Max r.i.p. 2/28/2018)

02-28-20

NOT FADE AWAY

a lifetime in comparative linguistics
a career in historical phonology
in echo reverberation and memory
seasons with troubadours singing new loves
thumbing through files and verb charts
irregularities of conjugation and grief
isolated one by one the vowels in intensive care
nuance of honorific pronouns in Spanish and Sanskrit
voyages of mystic Sinbads across unbidden seas
bearing on the shoulders not Anchises
but his troubled son to the ends of the earth
year after year of the big empty
the crevices and moon-scapes and bedlam
watching carefully for signs of aphasia
for the dot-tot-dot of the green ventilator
for the tubing and cross-hatches and sirens
the doo-wop of medical analysis
wire tapping and false dissemination of truth
the again and again of transfusion and elocution
how many lives in a single elapsed month
hiring and firing slaves for non compliance
a curriculum vitae of dialectology and nonsense
riding the fall ! is everything just a picture ?
dog-eared albums of photographic accident
steam rollers and brick paved streets of nostalgia
come home ! it keeps being pre-dawn
darkness of the waking animal
tired of sleeping of eating of dressing the wound
profundities of the oracular voice

ascending from its chewed leaf and madness
the real *sun* is the one never to rise again !
black is the horizon where it all goes
lexicon and verbiage of the nursing home
one after another consonants that diverge
there is no standard language ! only armies
jealous of imaginary boundaries
the world is distance and distance is unseen
the number of times we spent waiting
for someone for anyone to explain *why*
not fade away !

02-29-20

AN ACCOUNT OF THE RAZING OF THE *TEMPLE*

the scribblers musicians who can't read a note
archivists of dust dream-interpreters blind drunk
at the wheel fate-given soothsayers oracular palmists
the whole lot knocking at the door asking the dark
for entry & who was that peregrine soul just fled
jazz-timed for a cycle of light free-wheeling high
above the adjectival responses to life-on-earth
exploding ampersands that demand silence
of the still moving apostrophes and then night
the bewildering enfolds all beings in its embrace
rock and stone and tumultuous forms of sand
shores littered with the ruined cities of salt
brine and truss and flying spear-heads of envy
the fortuitous and less than blessed newly dead
the wounded hyphens and bric-a-brac pronunciation
of the words for *mother* and *soul* and the sirens and
gravity of cosmic demolitions everything flying
off its allotted spot on the *great picture* and stars
whose only minute is noon and the immense horses
glistening swart with dawn's liquid diamonds and
for why ? and what cacophonous battles of hair
and wrist and the amazons who come running
out of the lexicons of obscurity to dazzle the moment
with an exercise of vowels from the orient but
ever the absence of the One and the sequence of moons
bedeviled in their aspirin intensity and the weeping
in the woods the bereft hamadryads half clad

in rags of opulent silk and Chinese inks the quivering
and shaking of the epidermis oiled and sleek ready
for the grammar lesson of air and sun-spoil and
higher still the great Vedic Wheel with its butter-axle
and the sounds of archaic wisdom bright as lightning
in the rent cloud-work of the Epiphany rippling
through the everlasting hour that follows death
and the One and his retinue of plastic toys and owls
hide and seek between the swift-pacing Mountains
that emphasize the longing for twilight far off
where lunar tides elevate their sibylline tempests
and when prayers for Silence scatter their cold flares
a universe has come and gone and others more futile
will follow and the abracadabra of Mind click and woof
shuttering the thought-spectrum a maze of shot
words and parts of words and inflections of echo
a last leaf a grief the tender and darkness finally
and the disyllabic hiatus of eternity AOI

03-01-20

AT THE TOMB OF MEMORY

last lacking least the hour divided by years
as long as and even if the shade devours its
own light with grief the leaf diminished and
air turns for a moment sulfurous the depths
kenned in the slightest move an inch to the far
of the mountain beyond the realms of hungry
ghosts the sandy shores of where the fractions
and sky broken in spine by two doubled welkin
traversing as a comet's recall of fire dubious
who will do the talking back and forth whether
to proceed with as planned the epic counsel
murmuring others in their unsteadfast eddies
each a foot and dips it into the murk and loses
if for an instant balance and all reason flies
from thought a spite of vision the eye scours
its own backdrop and camps on the turf by
where there the horses trace the grassy knolls
it is a kind of rejuvenation the heavens open
a door and clouds of recollection the bright
spur of hope an afternoon in heat summering

quest for infinity in a spear of grass split
in uneven halves the both on their gravel shake
a future seeds spill and the highway manifests
trucks that churn oiled by night's suspect turn
hail ! a regard of painted warriors in stealth
the everyday becomes the illusion of movement
to and fro between the trees assigned to speech
even as the fading crest of day and barking
distances the unbidden dogs the haunted lees
mulch and underfoot defiles the dark place
that is hell's brief entrance and sorrowing loud
the voices yearning for the never been a past
of sacred rites of smokes and churlish desires
if a woman appears and the length of mourning
becomes biennial like dawn's rosy streak
then alas who are we attending this tumulus
a hill of mind the absences mount in number
sainted fragments of walk and creases deepen
brush and toil the famished event languishes
eternity is in that solemn fix of breath and
the rest a remote noise in the dusky leaves

03-02-20

FOSSILS OF LIGHT

seen floating the mind of clouds
streaming adjectives of dismissal
and regret the clauses formed by
thunder the aggravations of wheels
loosed from rambling god-chariots
the plus account of a dead deity
in his bed of heat and gravity
and decay in the fuses that spark
both end and beginning of the cosmos
a wonder we can think to *know*
when darkness wraps its heavy
linen around our shoulders and
setting forth on a single ray a beam
no greater than the size of grief
the inks and constabulary of reason
depravities of the urge to succeed
we remain half visible at the door

lessened by what we have forgotten
and little consoled by sensation
of the sun seeping into consciousness
to learn to divide the days into
balance and fraction and separating
the told from the untold somehow
develop memory as a category
of the intellect when it is nothing
more than rock fragment or crystal
mythiform and deictic particles
of air and leaf and the rushing
underground of the dead talking
wanting back their shadows
fossils of light

03-03-20

CUORE MATTO

Vita che piange, Morte che cammina
    Sergio Corazzini

Il cuore matto
Che ti vuole bene
Il cuore matto
Matto da legare

jukebox in the dusky Appenines
somewhere between the times of phonetic decay
and the desultory declining grammar of the hills
a signal from afar longing and despond
over the last stanzas dedicated to the *Unknown Love*
not come home again not find the path out
through the lengthening shadow of eternity
it's this way not that it's that way not this
stone over stone for centuries and phlox on the slope
and marginal ruins temple fragments smoking
faintly azure in the nave of memory
able to hear only a few echoes issuing from rock
granite arms of emperors astride horses enormous
as the palladium of abandoned gods
how many times left to harvest before it all burns out ?
I am this cipher this figment caught like an insect
between the tyrannical wheels of the oracle

what are years within this shaking leaf ?
immobility and blindness of the planet Mercury
noontimes resonant with seas of volcanic ash
adrift in fields of asphodel and yellow skies
will never return to the place of the bells
the campanile five in the afternoon reticent
after so many months of oratory and shouting
there is no right way no discernment of the future
nothing but the cabal of sibylline utterances
philology ! debates of accent tone and harmony
irregularities in grief and sorrow leading into
never out of the volcano with its legends of Persephone
not once but hundreds of times kidnapped !
if we chance to meet one another again
eking our paths down the steep of a bewildering lexicon
words and flutes and asterisks all lost in the air
heat returning in ever more immense cycles
decibels of a supreme descant the clouds !
should we ever chance an encounter again
and I at a loss to wonder why that should be
cuore matto ! tell me the truth though I will
never understand the dialects of ear and grass
and the speech acts of antiquity a ruin of sound
aphasia and the cataracts of divination
why ? it is a hotel of fog and gas a wreckage
by the Via Appia of twenty carriages piled up
the mangled dross of philosophy spinning in the brief
and the always silence of the inexplicable

Il cuore matto
Che ti vuole bene
Il cuore matto
Matto da legare

recorded by Little Tony, 1967

AN AFTERNOON ON MOUNT PARNASSUS

it's brief but was it bright the after-
noon on Parnassus the flocks of overhead
ominous in flight wings of royal birds
take-off but no delivery the street below
the façades colored with flapping awnings
fruit vendors or surgeons it's all the same
we came and went though revolving doors
a clinic at a time and lessened the sun's
hourly progress by the distance between
thumb and index finger shadows irregular
and unpronounceable personae called out
and vowels almost iridescent on the fade
hills of longing residue of grass and underfoot
the parallels that join the opposite ends
of space hearing but not listening to the loud
and intransigent noise of radios hand-held
the sidewalks trussed up with zombie crowds
traffic of motorized gods and the waning
sutures of voices reciting archaic hexameters
how was it longing and not its reverse grief
and the waiting rooms piled up with envelopes
of hair and combs the bristling identities of
pharmacists and the colloidal reducts of sorrow
plain-chant and prayers and Mariolatry pre-
scribed and patients ruminating on the other
side the task of light brought to bear on the
article of faith the dot and the squiggle and sign
of a hieroglyph the puzzle enervating enough
that brings life to its unwanted conclusion
and to sleep in stone and dream in inky graphs
the circling incidents of planet and ampersand
the insectary where we are bidden to live
the leaf that dwells in the shaking heart at
one with the fiery dust of the origins

03-07-20

YET HAVE THOU PITY AT LEAST
ON THE REST OF THE ACHAEANS

I'm not in high school any more
I've crossed the simple threshold
that places me closer to the end than
to the source of light much closer
to the depths where circles disappear
closing the archaic and the eddying pools
whirling the despondent verse into magma
the nothingness let's face it painted
on the wall to resemble a vase of calla lilies
when it must have been the year 1943
the last in the epidermis of infancy
revolves and spins the fast ever so high
the ebullient gone like dull chrome
songs of a music too tiny to record
and I am days past the inch that held
back the passage of numbers and space
the fixity of detail words alone and only
the stuff of thought going back and not
recalling why exactly to the opening
phrase *Arma virumque cano* incantation
of a springtime without boundaries
the lark singing sweetly in his small Latin
the girls too and the drugstore I am
over all that the trumpet hidden in
the leaf the discordant note and night
the unbidden with its enormous traffic
of pure silence I am beyond that now
perfume and cashmere sweaters and
hair ribbons and plate-glass windows
but where are the insects of the field
and the heat of the Roman emperors
in the corrupted series of events called
history opened to any page and read aloud
the vast and unintelligible volume of dates
and nomenclature and myth and nymphs
whose hair never dries the illustrated
edition of *Mind* and the deictic particles
meant to separate distance and proximity
and stars the dust and embolisms of longing
only grief has the upper hand now loss and

the small town where so much happened
in a matter of minutes and echoes
trellis and river bank of adolescence
and the roaring remote of the highway
traveling the invisible with its deaths
and their hieroglyphs the resonant last
of the darkening shroud of grass
I've crossed the simple threshold
it is the *Beyond* I already inhabit

03-08-20

AND HE FELL FROM HIS CAR AND HATEFUL DARKNESS GOT HOLD OF HIM

not the wooden sword and shield
painted with its motto in backwards
red and the shine and bright of each
blade of grass yearning for a new day
in the furious afternoon of time nor
even the twilight in the mouth and
the sliding abacus of inevitability when
the decision was made to go ahead
and excavate the puerile mind fragile
for its want of experience and light
what a day ! a thousand and one sailors
abandoned on a single wave-scourged rock
would you ever see a perfect noon again ?
questions that leave no marks in sand
ropes and hawsers and twill and darning
such is the ravel of your gone time
on an earth too illusory to hold you
for long in its embrace of absent arms
even though your singular hand shaped
a great air and a sky attached to it as
an afterthought of a cosmos gone wrong
what a day ! a museum made of glass
and distance a roaming walkway darker
than the time you went to sleep on the
other side of the lunar bed your head
wrapped in the gauzy circumference
of aphasia and dazzling ampersands
enough ! someone has shoved the last

two years into a thimble forgetting
to write the prescription for waking
leaving us bewildered as to which chasm
to expect for your small voice to emerge
replete with the uninflected nouns of
nursery rhymes and leaves struggling
to recall the vanishing speech of dew
what a day ! what a truly remarkable day !
and you alone you who hold the secret
of its imperishable hour of eternity

Max, 52 years

03-09-20

NELLA SELVA OSCURA

I cannot name this wood this forlorn
viaticum these shadows in dense retreat
though I have been here time and time again
and beyond the knitted wharf of leaves
where the archaic sun abandons his car
for the dusky steeds of memory and aloft
the timber of burning constellations unnamed
for the unremembered dead who went ahead
thinking there must be a place in the remotest
where gathering all the adjectives and signs
a quadrant exists where all lives rejoin
in a hand-dance of mournful rhapsody
but alas no such mark persists in tilted space
and above the streak of still-born dawn
seems to glow a day such as this come no more
inkling of childhood fused to a marble floor
hair unkempt as blossoms in Dravidian verse
alone this last of beings I am and wander such
in curtailed hexameter of friends gone lost
in hills of chalky grammar and founts ancient
as stone and the immemorial river-bend where
the knees of a first experience doubled in grief
and upon the erstwhile shoulder perched
the irreverent bird of omen and dead sooth
so many other hints and taints the winds scoured
I no more the student of pure philology but
aghast at the broken gate I stand trembling

which hand to hold which key to use this
of mold and star-flung shape grown dun
or the formless one the rust of libraries
books and parchments gone to inch and dust
powders of the orient ! words that were
never used and sounds of echoes unemployed
to open what ? the vast and empty lore
of consonants littering the skies with histories
of rock fragments without meaning the fade
and trace of fossils and twilit mountain crags
to turn around and shut the deep with its fields
of voided thought and sleeping immensities
do we have any idea of who and why we are ?
snared in this Merovingian labyrinth of dark
and spun around and tossed the merest mind
itself goes astray bewilderment and nerve
light an abject puzzle in the vanishing firmament
from this wood I cannot remove the loss
and grieving yellow sorrow in the leaves
alone in this fierce dank swirl, *to breathe !*
the all a slender syllable the shape of air
escaping from the unknown woof of time

03-09-20

A SMALL LOTUS SUTRA

the days of autobiography are over
name things for what they are
a sun a rock an accident and death
nouns are verses made of one line
memory depleted of its oceanic surges
separate the threads if possible
return nothing to the source but let
things wander loosened of their fit
space is outside the span of thumb
and index and the urge to employ
metaphor whenever possible canceled
a legend is what flutters in the light
depths and heights and the sudden
loss of a body cause mourning
if you see something running across
the field or a cloud in transit above

the fine line that divides bright
from darkness or if you no longer
care to discern movement in its
most distinct hues but rather lie
down and let breath take its course
this is renunciation of mind the brief
intaglio in constant flux of thought
how sincere the denial of the door
when something rings don't pick it up
the echo will linger and the fade
of inactivity on the wall a mark
that puzzles before it vanishes utterly
but never try to fix the broken shade
instead let transverse the planets fall
from their destinies across the lamp
for they are nothing but fireflies confused
in their ambition to control gravity
all things are at once annihilated
and the sounds of names and the vowels
lodged between certain consonants
these are matters for the ear alone
and sleep the densest admission
that one cannot keep going on into

03-10-20

A COURSE IN CLASSICAL PHILOLOGY

dark Lady-of-Corruption into thy bosom et cetera
modernism one step away from its own funeral
blistering and high the tropes deepening wounds
grief I splinter into thirds the least of which
when they returned all they could say was *The Nymphs!*
of the college and of the wasteland the distances
toward the river's exacerbated dumps the mire
and morass which they call tragedy and moon-shine
how they flit the vagabonds of hope in rags and
chamois cloth and raise their broken arms to
a puerile deity a faun a discarded angelic niche
steer clear of the Sirens lay no claim to Echo!
as no other day this is the one the cosmos sinks
into its own detritus and star flakes and ampersands
burning as they fall what phrase what romantic

illusion to fill the parent of sleep with darker still
and clouds looming in the ranks of speech syllabic
entries in the booking wistful night-like whispers
into the mind's great corollary Stone and do pronouns
forsake their shape and shadows groomed for ecstasy
simply vanish in the camps of grieving grass ?
the time of afterthought and foreboding the instant
of Recognition and the scampering idiot thoughts
that make of art a canvas blanketed in asbestos
to speak French as Rimbaud ! so declare the denizens
of post-modernism and the poetics of slam and
the rudimentary art of sailing through hexameters
has been lost to fiber-optics and search engines
physiology of light and pataphysics of grounded sound
dialects of the ear ! how many distinctions contained
in the schwa and the failing pluperfect tense alas
decry the humiliated of the grammar class whose leafy
talk adumbrates through long riverine afternoons
dreams like formless waves and tides scour mortal
consciousness yet bring to bear nothing on the rock
standing in the middle of sorrow and the skies that
hail upon the chastened bower glimmerings of alpha
so much and yet nothing else that matters the edge
is all the skimmings on the margin of half-words
implosions of illicit vowels the ambergris of seers
when half as much has eluded perception and
the rest lies in tatters of consonants and cuneiform
what heuristics of philological madness *letters* !
understand nothing give in to air's pure brevity
lay the head down here beside the temple fragments
great Apollo will be back no more and dust eternal

03-11-20

THE ORIGINS OF POETRY IN SOUND

the largest was the dark tumor of sound
ascending from the valley a cluster of depths
the ear alone could in its sleep decode the vast
beyond comprehension all stood around and
horses by the hundreds elephants chariots maimed
the furious agitation of the clouds with their spears
of lightning and heron feathers and globes of immense
burning dust and the eyes of the gods incensed
and the slow ting-ting of temple bells in the welkin
and the chants and prayers of priests assigned
by color to the various castes of mortals defiled
and urged by passions into unreason and from
somewhere in the inch that separates the scarab
from its metropolis the tempestuous winds
streaked with saffron and sandalwood tearing
from the roots great banyan and baobab trees
sacred for their immobility over the centuries
and did none have insight to step out of illusion ?
lesser echoes tremolos from bamboo flutes
or merely the carelessly abused vowels of mind
aflutter to organize *Thought* to no avail even
as the black sun rising from its serpentine night
thrust its unbridled steeds of pure glistening swart
and indignant over the meridian and crashing
envelopes of atmosphere and the luster of eons
shuddered for an instant only in a cataract
of stupendous consonants dividing and dividing again
speech from the malpractice of men leaving space
wide open to conjectures of dissolution and loss
+ + + + + + + + + + + + + – + + + + + + + + + + + + + + + +
thus it was one day out of time , the poets
inventors of craft and lies described the tumult of noise
arising from the seed and its immolation under
the names of kings dynasties and seas
all of history recorded and unrecorded reduced
to the drifting pollen gorgeous yellow billowing
from flower to flower in the polyvalent silence
proceeding from the dense hive of time and sleep

03-12-20

ADOLESCENCE

the one who approaches and the one who draws away
the self-same shadow shared the self-same spirit gone
was the alternate day in time the last but one
and turned to look into the fray blossom against blossom
the mighty air that swirled taking from breath the life-glimpse
suddenly metal lost its sheen and sun darkened in the blare
an elephant danced on a lotus fanning its delicacy across
the expanse of night and from a thousand spinning cars
heroes vaunted for their pedigree flung their last
a shower of gold-tipped shafts in clouds high into the blue
whose cry was heard and whose muffled in the monstrous din
waves of dust crowns of imitation moons none could discern
the limbs of glory the shield and ax and ornaments of jade
and onyx the prayers in spoken cuneiform to the goddess
the severed hands still jubilant in the winds still talking
ceasing to take shape and mind's faint recall of the bookstore
where its youth emerged in countless pages of oneiric shift
girlfriends gathered beneath the four-faced clock that
hung above the drugstore and panoply of weights and
adolescence how futile the regard in sandstone of the library
the traffic and avenues of budding intellect to separate
in the midst of carillon and roaring dots the *one* idea
of the dance and its corollaries of ampersand and grief
did pass in a single burning instant from foot to shoulder-blade
the promised life the vagrant splendors of immortality
and flashing in the blazing eye eternity's tiny monuments
names and egos and fin and hoof the passage of lovers
immutable inconstancies and the tombstone of regrets
how swift the leaf came to speech and swifter still
the darker wing of silence put to an end all sound

03-13-20

PROLEGOMENON TO THE SCOURGE

the sacred and unlimited rock
is but a shadow cast upon unseen waters
were we but children in a storybook again
the fleeting moments like honey on the leaf
and the plagues and sores of human plight
but distant errors on the spatial margin
yet here we stand on the verge of this abyss
and call the world an unfortunate spinning quoit
the pages we used to turn with fingers
agile as grass in the yielding wind
are but cinders scattered in desolate air
to one another strangers we are become
the nestled flute the once radiant river-bend
equal nothing in our fevered passing dream
the shapes of continents like the size of mountains
but wavering sequences of dots and squiggles
languages that come and go through reed
and banyan root and baskets full of plums
resound with ancient vowels heard in twilight
sleep the renunciation of mind the smallest elbow
crooked in the feather-down all a mystery
of appearance and memory
what has ever been an echo of names fading
as hues in the dawn's fragile dew
and even the great god sun an illusion
of bright and fiery nothingness
his chariot of melting butter his steeds
of pure sweat and indignation
the abyss into which he plunges nightly
one day never to return again
we are *this* and *that* we like to say
but which is the *one* unless it is the *other*
futile paradigms of grammar and wit
the sounds we hear the things we taste
the shapes we see shimmering lovely in a trance
are bitter gifts the tricks of death
who stands at the end his mouth all-devouring
his right hand on the *staff* and
his left bandaged with eternity

03-14-20

ECHOES

dust in blossoms darkness and illumination
walls of fire triggered by small desires
the eye and all it perceives an instamatic lens
down to valleys of hidden sound and up to peaks
where nothing lasts not even air in its multiple density
alphabets and triggers and drugged overlords
the world's infinitesimal history in a thumbnail
dulcet tones the lyre of infancy the blown
clouds in a pod of yellowing saffron underneath
which is the myth of the sun drying on its trellis
bosoms heavy with the plaint of goddesses
who govern the tiny ruins of birth and destiny
a hand was given once to a round of vowels
and fingers woven between the sleep of grasses
ancient as ever the loud tympanum in the rock
trying to wake the mind from its dream
nothing advances the foot from its horse
nor the hair-line where evidence of beauty lies
all afternoon anxiously awaiting the door
and if it opens only to reveal a sky of emptiness
stars and quadrilles of noontime punctuation
statues denied their mortality and gods roaming
the lonesome stone of the unconscious sea
how do names become ? what is matter ?
space comes round to its small dot aquiver
expecting the big bang to boom thrice again
and children the size of bees alert to color
and to the depths within a single leaf
and flowers known to last a minute and planets
carved out of a drop of ink ! grammars of memory
interred in the plot of earth numbered zero
how much and how many do we have to earn
before suffering and its joyous death are ours
to embrace in the fever of our oblivion ?

03-15-20

THESE DAYS

can the inflections of ancient words instruct us
can grief be parsed and conjugated for person number
voice and tense and what are the margins of sound
echolalia of rock formations irregularities of light
resonance of seas that have been forgotten by
the voyagers who have sailed their tempestuous surface
only to return to a destruction of consonants
hard by the ravaged wood and the dry well
is language obsolete syllable by syllable plundered
by grammarians of elegance and style oblivious
of the sorrow and inchoate ruin buried in each
archaic vowel and what is it we are after when Zeus
implodes before our very eyes in dereliction of robes
and saffron bolts stammer through the heavens
announcing in a voice borrowed from early radio
abandon the Noun ! mortals you are no more
than statuary bereft of accent and tone marble
hewn from the idea of immortality and thrust aside
into ditches where in your sleep you continue warbling
threats and innuendo envy of the gods of dustless feet
and so on was there ever a first day of innocence ?
fingers of chalk held up to test the wind's directions
nothing returns of formalized declension case and number
pronouns stagnate from over-use and the honorific
employed to address the supreme entity shrivels
on its slender reed of winnowed air and the Ear !
what can it hear but phonetic decay and lunacy
distances of half an inch and landslides taking thumb
and shoulder of the continents into seething waters
it is a dumb-bell and a crown and a steeple magnified
by the lens of unreason and atmospheres loud
in their catastrophic rush to end the planetary ellipse
children ! the day of the hieroglyph and colored ampersand
is here and the rambling song of unknown alphabets
and above all the shapes and wild abstractions
of the earliest poetry grass and leaf and stream
all a shimmer in the afternoon's perfect instant
if only you were *all* still alive to memorize these
stanzas of bliss and eternal silence

03-16-20

AFTER ALL THIS TIME

first of all I miss Joe it's hard to believe
I am 81 and he isn't I keep seeing life
as a series of fitful half-sleeps little glimpses
into sunlit lawns lying on our backs
supposing the airplane droning overhead
belongs to Uncle Vernie though he
crashed in his in the jungles of WWII
turning on our sides a map develops
the full street labyrinth of Los Angeles 1945
and someone is pronouncing one of us
dead he checked out at 72 too young for
a cartographer with a degree in mystification
numerologist and skilled at climbing
pyramids a sun or moon at a time and
together in another half-sleep playing
with snow for the first time we exchange
over and over again face and voice and
use the radio for a great imagination
of the cosmos almost 9 years full since
he pulled out of the race leaving me
bewildered in that alley of discovery
around 10 years of age when we started
dividing the world between us as depicted
on the colored pages of an atlas made in 1903
I got London and he got Paris and so on
together in another half-sleep that pulled
us out to a river-bank and named things
for what they weren't an edge to the sky
a bolt of azure cloud fragments lazily
sliding across an enormous light wondering
if when we got home things would be different
the quiet end to mom's utterances or fear
that dad would come home too soon so
I am lying here in half-sleep alone not
knowing when exactly but the wall-paper
with its tropical islands adrift in the sepulcher
of thought and Joe wandering between waters
and palm-fronds and making drzzzzzz noises
as if he were a dive bomber coming to
wake mankind out of its torpor and it's
hard to discern what life it is in what yard we

are still playing and whose got whose shirt
on backwards and walking together under
a beastly summer sun on a lone highway
that leads anywhere but to death especially
and can it really be that anything at all
has ever happened that we grew up and distant
and pell mell old scores of music shattered
lines from poetry we shared and library books
with pages torn and dates of illustration
cameo reflections of the afterbirth and so
on and so on in our leather jackets smirking
trying hard not to cry or feel a sense of panic
sitting Sundays on cold church pews while
the minister rattles on about the death
after life the one Joe has inhabited since
2011 the year before his great panorama
and revelation leaving me only half the *other*
I was born with and at 81 waiting for the
phone to ring and you know who with
the same voice as mine in eternity

03-17-20

THE WORLD AS IT IS

the beatific moment when air realizes
it has come to an end and gravity with
its immense hands of fortune and destiny
has no more domain and the small circling
dot by turns azure and vermillion is about
to expire in a longitude of heat and ire
this is where we are with small memories
of budding branch and dew smitten lawns
grasses in all their innocent simplicity
bowing to the invisible deities of wind
and rain and childhoods too bent like twigs
in an errant hour of tempests and sun-bright
come along to the edge where water once
crystalline now moves sluggishly inert
not the capacity for light and reflection
but the dangerous mass of rising tropics
rest here the weary stone and its worm
to which shore do we aim our riddled bark

and with which withered flowers adorn
the mottled marble of the disdained goddess
section by section the paper heavens
on which were once painted constellations
with smoking and wondrous names myth
and sword and steed alike in a rush
to convert history to its pointillistic dust
begin to curl burning slowly asterisk and
ampersand planets and ink-blots and fuses
ready to go off in the midnight ear of rock
dusky mind ! at which point do you turn inward
in another failed attempt to read the map !
today is a repetition however untranslatable
of the oracle a mimesis and silent echolalia
of something we all must have read at birth
coming into being and puzzled at the going out
maze and miasma of names and sounds
vowels thrust into the red and consonants
clustered at gunpoint to resound in sleep
dreams of masks exchanging roles and speech
excoriations of syllable and punctuation
utter babble and aphasia of the lost city
children ! listen and watch this diorama
fading mountain paths and running shorelines
how many the hues in a single ray of light ?
through which gate did the Buddha exit ?

03-18-20

THE ARCHAIC MOMENT

"afin que vif et mort ton corps
ne soit que roses"
    Ronsard

the first bud the rose of may
will it ever bloom again
it's childhood's trance the light
a folly of multicolored days
the maze of noise and winged
things that make of noon delight
the summer spray of bright array
the leaf with its pointed speech
the thousand-screened empire of grass

the footfall in the stone's small ear
the brain with its city maps and
conduits and viaducts and rout
can it bear to relive its memory
of lawns and slopes of emerald glare
a fuse and its disarray of nights
grief's plenitude of fallen stars
jewelry of all the poems forgotten
in the mists where seas used to be
alarms in the hand's tiny rain and
echoes of the eyelid shutting
over the porphyry of mind
the tender sapling and its child
playing with the wheels of Fate
the thread and its red labyrinth
a season yellowing beside the wall
winds that take the shape of gods
and gods whose misstep is eternity
all the corollaries of thought
in the cosmic magnitude of sleep
and still we listen for the glass
to break and the stain to spread
across infinity's budding infancy

03-19-20

OLVIDOS DE MI PADRE

para mi hermana

I fell asleep in my father's arms
though dead he's been more than 20 years
I nestled in his reek of disguised alcohol
shaving lotion old spice tropic fantasy
it's easy to forget just how hard it was
to earn his love and companionship
exile that he was with Guadalajara hair
a faint curse was ever on his lips
for the routines of Lutheran synecdoche
and sarcasm dripped constantly
in the twinkle of his cinematic eyes
still I burrowed in his post meridian clasp
a whole afternoon with his lemon drops
and Mexican newspaper headlines
in and out of oils and acrylics on canvas

street names for unknown saints and
incense burning dense as beeswax in the air
distance was his propriety and music
with Saint John of the Cross at 3 AM
blear-eyed from bar-hopping bouts
and mornings wrapped in tortilla dough
he hustled remote as a pyramid of oil
through days of anathema and dialect
how could I in his embrace ever fall
curtail my living self in his promised death
full hours of plight and anguish smoking
decks of pall mall cigarettes his hand
unwavering holding the subtle brush
to splash color over an unwrapped thought
a cathedral a half-dead donkey colonial
houses muffled in Aztec silver-work
filigree of bluish haze his archaic skies
riddled with recollections of a mountain
and the immense purple mysteries
of a Tenochtitlan buried in Toltec grief
winding sheets and Amarillo sweat dying
the ruffled edges of his floating bed
his caravanserai of forbidden paramours
a theater of nickel soaps and pulque
the brash despair of his uprooted life
going in circles long Sunday afternoons
when ennui put on a German mask
deriding the colloquy of his solitude
but to nuzzle up to his bristling breath
and die a hundred times just for once
before his own soul took to flight
five thousand miles from his birth
that crazy Mexican of elegance and ire
how far however far from the painted rocks
and shifting gravel of his planned walk-away
only the broken vowels of his idiom
the consonants of cactus and parakeet
cajole my drowsing ear this ancient day
when the whole world tilts drowning
in a gold-fish bowl and darkness overtakes
drowns in a gold-fish bowl
and darkness overtakes

03-19-20

A ROADSIDE EPITAPH

which is the cup and which is the horse
in the white sheets of this conflagration ?
the one toy was a rain drop the other
a spinning top with voice of an oracle
to look but once was to be deceived
to listen alone was to hear the volume
of eternity rushing into its own finale
what was to touch and who was to be ?
memory set aside from its hush of leaves
without origin or shape a flash of green
before surrendering to the clouds of sleep
life on earth is it but a passing moment ?
hummingbird and bee a squall of echoes
names scrambled in the fold of lost vowels
chance and light like storms in the eye
desperate skies traveling without their gods !
what is perpetual if not the silent note ?
mourn for the donkey you flogged to death
grieve for the stone removed at twilight
the inch of the cathedral the frame of bright
ten times the size of ink in its turbulence
what else happens in the transcendent moment
when matter supersedes itself with dust ?
panoply of consonants in the taciturn blur
which is the increment of childhood loss
how long the twist and how brief the curve
the road most worn but never traveled !
a finger up to hail the stranger a bandage
and a saddle and places like small pools
filling with the water of the moon and
whose face is the guest in glass and whose
tired head now stills the roaming grass
this is the end of time , My Friend ,
this is the very end of time on earth

03-20-20

GIORNATA DELLA POESIA

which came first—death or memory ?
lilies gilding the famous pathway to the stars
a hand an ovation at a time a smaller cusp
of rain a system of air with sand drills
the ever absent city of children playing rope
the seas already lost in a monotony of echo
and a landscape of mountains forever asleep
poesia ! shadow of noise ! this is your day
nations of leaf and skeleton of fossil clouds
of attributes steep as cliff or soft as marauding
silks in the fists of unknown lovers who dwell
in the beyond of verse and phantom rhyme
poesia ! labyrinth of rumors riddled in rock
regrets that myth and nymph are only hair
shaken out wet to dry in an oriental sun
fuses of dream ivy and hoarse skies
gods who only now have learned to read
loud sequence of vowels and anthems
heavens blossoming like lotuses in dark pools
that are nothing more than punctuation and meter
brief are the colors red and azure the dots
parading around the brow of the grieving *goddess*
this is your day ! statehood of the oracular aleph
trumpet-vine and liquor of the unbegun verse
women and dance and grammar all
involved in the constructs of beauty divine
recited and memorized and forgotten in
the single afternoon of incomplete marble
poesia ! pronoun of the honorific bed
detail in the meridian of sound that occurs
every noon when no one is listening but for
the grasses running to seize the wind's skirts
and flee and flee again ! poetry is narcolepsy
the wish to return where there is no space
no Dravidian subdivision of consonant and tone
where stone is buried in stone and light
a fleeting glimpse into the alternate Hour
poesia ! farewell to the mortal moment
goodbye to the coffin and its pictograms
the dead ! the immemorial dead and their lawn
that inch of seizure and inks on the edge

where the unconscious becomes all
which came first—death or memory ?

03-21-20

TULIPS

joe and ivan

spring 1953 marveling at the first budding tulips
protruding through winter's lingering snowbed
seasons change ! time zones all aflutter with sameness
and diversity continents in upheaval glaciers
and rainforests turning on a dime the world !
as it were a province in the pockets of the twins
those idiomatic ashplants wandering smalltown
all eyes and ears to the sky's fluted birdsong
yellow the streaks left behind by gods being born
for the second or third time in a new adolescence
metals and hues of archaic rock and sandstorms
that flood the eye with literatures and pyramids
walking the thin dotted line between life and death
the grammar books of pure air and primavera
breezes that denuded unimaginable statues of
rain and nymphs whose secret lives consisted of
island names too difficult to pronounce and sirens
weaving a spell of unheard notes in the small space
that swells between the first numbered street and
its clinic and the masses of inchoate hills yearning
for delivery from history and a return to myth
plenitude of color ! it was time to start painting
and writing turning each emotion into a syllabic
display of innocence and its opposite annihilation
sing aloud the chants of the underground and what !
rounding each corner careful not to step on demons
the size of ink lurking to take the mind with alcohol
and behold *that* day with its blossoming snowflowers
turns into a lifetime later busy and labyrinthine
the mind's multiple and incoherent city maps
unfurled and sent whizzing past Saturn and Uranus
galaxies of portfolio in Quechua and Toltec distances
did the world allow for time to be so infinitely diminished ?
how could the one be at such a remote from the other ?
upside down with masks borrowed from Etruscan graves

everything written backwards now without mirrors
to read the immense finger of fate moving cloud-like
through the millennial dusts and oddly enough
going back to springtime 1953 and the unseen hands
of light and fragrance and the wonder inherent
in dying at the very moment of self-discovery

03-22-20

ON THE DEATH OF *VALUM VOTAN* 9 YEARS ON

i

no clinic carillon pealing the 5 o'clock rounds
brassy resonance in the fading southern sky
no forest murmur alert no five high flute notes
nor pale echo of cave or hillside grotto shades
to lay down heavy the head with distance filled
its memories escaping to no known source
imminent unending night of ink-black stars
adieu ! *frater hermano fratello frère Bruder*
most ancient of sounds the invisible vowels
detached from all consonance and harmony
epic center in the middle of nowhere dying
a great but unknown Latin hexameter winding
around either wrist and a pang of Vedic OM
where the throat becomes a dusky piece of air
all breath sent forth into the unseen integers
that join number and space to eliminate time
no more photographs of motels in dusty neon
Carretera Panamericana bearing your self
to spin in the ruins of Yucatan the calendar
your fate commingled with a tex-mex jukebox
playing Kitty Wells *Repenting* hung-over and
thirsting for the one moment of pure clarity
birth and death in an instant in the snows
zigzagging wildly half conscious into the Tree
of knowledge and to wake just once again
in the late half-hour of eternity a twin
beside his twin listening to the archaic radio's
magical voices of distance and oblivion

ii

when did we learn to count to add multiply divide
and then to Subtract !

iii

Aśvinā, twins and inseparable
young and ancient bright lords of luster
of golden brilliance and adorned with lotus garlands
they are the only gods called golden-pathed
strong and agile fleet as thought
possessed of profound wisdom and occult power
they are dasrá (wondrous) and nāsatya (true)
they desire honey and are drinkers of it
they poured out a hundred jars of honey
their car is honey-hued and honey-bearing
and they are compared with bees
their car passes over the five countries
and moves around in the sky
they abide in the sea of heaven but
sometimes their locality is unknown
they appear between dawn and sunrise
dispelling darkness and evil spirits
their physical basis has been a puzzle
for they are half light and half dark*

iv

poetry of nine and square root of three
numerologist supreme *Valum Votan* !
in either hand the columns of smoke and days
how far traveled from the high school rout
from the buoyancy of hills to sleep and dawns
when the last green stars are seen fleeing
were you here today how would you practice
social distancing and refer all things to their lair ?
the morning you suffered the last trance
and without seeing saw it all in a great flash
I called out your name *My Brother*
and it was afternoon in a different continent
oceans and oceans away from your hearing
now nothing not even the slightest trace of that

*Adapted from *A Vedic reader for students*, A.A. Macdonell

golden honey-hued car in which we traveled together
across the small garden of sky looking
below at the furiously crumpled maps
earth the former paradise of bees and thought !

03-23-20

THE POEM I CEASED WRITING

"Prierai la Mort noircir mon plus clair jour"
  Louise Labé

the last time I wrote this poem the grass
was loud and clear and bright the skies
with their quadrilateral warning systems
and in the leaf I heard repeated the echo
of my silence the verses of sleeping marble
how infinite seemed the meter in the veins
the last time I read this poem and light
beams skirted the unconscious mind
pretending to wake from a troubled dream
aura and resonance of the preterit sea
and each hand a realm of divided shapes
of noontimes in a pool of dusky vowels
heights of drowsy splendor and vertigo
the words tumbling out like meteors
whatever they could pronounce or spell
meant nothing the last time I erased
this poem and stuck to the blanks and
dots of a distant hemisphere and voices
reciting what I never wrote and palms
read furtively in a black mirror signed
the air with fractured hieroglyphic
strokes the spirits of language gone
crazy and the stillness and departure
of the dead heading south to sunnyland
take this silver turban off my head !
to this end we speak 16th century French
and deploy the consonants in an array
of mountain peaks by the Adriatic shore
wherever the poem went with its syllabic
lore and depths is immaterial I won't
write it again and rest the remains of
memory with the child whose broken

nouns and incomplete irregular verbs
lie in the ashen grammar of far west
the occidental spine hidden in mists
of oracle and ire the mythic chords
meant to accompany this ruined poem
a series of reverberations in canyons
lost in the mind's dark cuneiform

03-24-20

TOBOGGAN

vowels hanging like icicles in the frozen night
dark as a mortuary at noon the heavens descend
promising nothing but the smothering glacier of air
in what amaze do the adolescents board the toboggan
a glee and a surfeit of joy whooping muffled
in the dense winter garb clambering on the narrow skiff
that wends its way down snow-terraced slopes
at the speed of thought and gliding ever faster
down the treacherous incline Lo who falls first
into the ditch but brother Joe with a merry laugh
and life suddenly turns its back and the woods
barely visible where haunted beasts blood-eyed
snarl growling with a nightmare menace
children ! don't look back the end is near
a thousand years will pass in this mirrored instant
high school yearbooks will burn and photos transgressed
by the lie of breath the handsome rectilinear
profiles the slicked hair the half-smile
of a weary docility behind which the mind's trickster
is at play in the domain of birth and illusion
Joe half buried in the white dust *knows*
that Spain is just half an inch away bleached
and doused in the cornet's brassy blare
dead donkeys and matadors and poisoned suns
soon it will be later in the afternoon meltdown
the world will have formed the path to its final days
the kids poised and posed for their great egress
pomaded and sated with cigarette and coke
will sit there waiting for the photographer's flash
which will never come even as the toboggan
slams to a finish against an irreverent pine

extending its blackened arms into the skies
which turn ever yearning for the dawn
and the green stars fleeing from the chaotic axle
diminish their lamps and disappear

03-25-20

LA FIN DU MONDE : CHANSON

the cold it was the winter my love
half a sky into immortality the frozen
weft of clouds invisible the my love
a garden to the other side of life
a springtime to come if ever again
my love the floral display in eyes
alone the greenery of the echo
distance in its ramparts of silence
and longing hills my love of grief
the thin equator that separates us
tropic hive of distilled honey the mind
in its outbreak of thought my love
to choose if we only could the breath
inherent in the playful child and my
love to snuff it when our backs are
turned the mountain in the window
the shares of infinity in the lambent
sun as it decks its car behind the mass
of porphyry shadow my love the end
of the world in unbidden syllables
the pools of grace the darkening eve
& night my love the stellar tomb

03-26-20

THE GRAMMATICAL ERROR

the serenity that comes when numbers
are freed of their debates and sleep the great
isolator and the ledges of cloud refined yet
troubled by their inherent grammatical error
and so much else that cannot be accounted for
the world in its diminishment a haze of waste-green air
and rampant unseen viruses and oracular
voices heard for whatever reason only at three AM
when the demons of ink and falsified passports
and the travelers who forsook the dream for
a falsified ticket and flight into the syllabic atmospheres
and speaking a token French and virtually blind
from hypnotic acts of jealousy the world-leader
pivots on an invisible crevice and how much
more is the daily briefing going to hide ?
insomnia and madness and adolescent prayer wheels
juxtapositions of metaphysics and ceramics
vowels and the obliterating nose-bleed of politics
and the wars in the sands and the rutilating noon
of an unnamed planet as it wheels dangerously
near the pagoda of irrelevance and salvation
dot dot dot the nuisance of radiophonic bedlam
innocence castrated on the internet and savage
consonants purloined and deafened by twilight
the why-go-on of the nay-sayers and the photo finish
of the Trojan horse hard by the Stygian vale
Oh dark thou art the knife of time ! shake it
demolish the codes of dust and ambiguity
answer to nothing but the purity of language
the thin crimson thread unraveling in sandalwood
and the break with the past and the forensic
knowledge of Mandrake the Magician
can it be that this really is the end ?

03-27-20

THE NEVER-ENDING SONG

eglantine and the bower where lovers hide
when pitch black the thunderous noon befalls
rains the constant of forty years and meadows
drenched in the archaic floods and flames
that sudden pierce the bloody welkin
'tis time to celebrate the novelty of life !
so say the mendicant rishis and jongleurs
chanting a psalm of lamps and dividends
shares in the breath of phantomatic beings
illusions abound ! when was there ever a season
so bright as song and the whiskbroom and the file
that eliminate the dust and patchwork air
let flash the new god's tooth and symbolize
the joys of grass and reeds the fluted sounds
the airs lapsed in languages of long gone
stone columns of mystery and reasons not
to sleep but wander o'er the rocky glade
in search of nymphs whose iridescent hair
a whole afternoon takes to dry and sunspots
and calla lilies painted on the forged sheets
that flap invisibly on the lines that separate
time from space and eager the souls just born
to navigate their unknown course projectiles
of vowel and accent and fingers counted
thrice over to assure the eye it's not to blame
and winds the size and shape of ink or sand
that take the lovers by surprise and write
in the antic storm a poem of never ending
yes and write the winds a poem of never ending !

03-27-20

COMP LIT I

where Ma Durga sits with Shiva
in an eternity of fireflies
the world appears simply one of many dots
crimson and sapphire by turns then fade
the loudest literature is in the mountain-script
a legend of echoes named Kabir and Dante
hell-trips and falsified sufi saints abound
and Ionian shores where Thetis grieves
and Apollo on his bright but dwindling sun-ray
comparisons between east and west the diphthongs
and vowels elongated to make hexameter
threnodies in perfect epic Sanskrit shatter
the pallid air and abundant as consonants may be
the Chinese landscape turns to watercolor flares
in faint azure and crystalline distances
when we used to say *the end of the world*
we meant it figuratively not as it really is
but today in our sheltered motels and sorrowing inns
in our Spanish palisades of deadly ice-rinks
in our Italian villas of non-stop crematoria
we know that the classes in comparative literature
the symposia and lecture series on Homer and the Avesta
the long train of afternoons sleeping in Lucretius
small dust storms and atomic theory and nation states
built on Machiavelli and Voltaire while rock fragments
on the border wall attest to empires come and gone
to Ashoka and Alexander and nameless Ming princes
the yawning altar of Cipango's brilliant rise
in silk and Murasaki diadems and et cetera
for everything we ever thought was clear and pure
chronologies and Jataka tales of Lord Shakyamuni
footnotes and bibliographies to establish Truth
all that's a sham a Pascalian diversion of the mind
it's where Ma Durga pivots on Shiva's lap
illusion of the Himalayan mountain peaks
the snows and fireflies of infinite regret
myths of deported gods and clouds rife with flame
the *this* of the *that* in coordinates of five
tutorials that divide eons between Vedas and socialism
the eternities inherent in the tonic accent and
the monotonous chant of PhDs in the recital hall

music ! bong ! bonzes who set themselves aflame
blind and naked rishis eating orange goop
stumbling across Dravidian ecstasies of Bang
what did we ever learn 4 years of liberal arts
semantics and quantum theory and democracy
of all things and now *the* today that is the last
what is to compare of the virtues of Arjuna
and the bedeviled brain of Prince Myshkin ?
we are in this little paper shell tossed
on the Sea-of-Being and lost in fogs of thought
anxiety and salvation and the small poetry
that puts the ear to sleep by day's end
not mortals but shadows of memory

03-28-20

POETRY : A CONFESSION

I am a force I am *the* force
if I were a mountain I would fly
petrel and lapwing jackdaw and jay
I ride the dark wing into the heavens
a song none can hear but the divinely dead
when you see the sun it is a mass of burning sheaves
whirlpools of flaming destruction an apocalypse
but all I see is the black center of time
a moment of loss and disappearance or hours
spent on the bench of Ulysses pondering
ever wondering where the island has gone
or I am Gautama discoursing back and forth
in ancient Pali about the shares and dividends of desire
births come and go events so monumental
they are forgotten in a trice when the next tsunami hits
I am a single thought giving birth to the world
a form of mind that is prepared to darken
with the shadows that govern outer space
a diadem a scruple a deity of hair and combs
beautiful things ravage me as they consume moons
and the skin of polyglot naiads fresh from the pools
lotus eyed the secret god who haunts me
ask for my heart back and to make music
with a single cat-gut string and to rejoice
because there is nowhere else to go

but off the cliff of earthly redundancies
to leap as if light and air were finally vanished
from the imagination that sustained vowels
for so many centuries of human endeavor and
myth and the rock formations on the edge of sleep
the eternal vicissitude of an echo looking for silence
harsh but numinous consonants devoid of harmony
the perpetual motion of an isolated number
vibrating at the source of ink not to speak
of the pyramid and the stone of its origins
and the wild heretical notion of water
all-surrounding the febrile peninsulas of history
a jagged tomb a swirl of alphabets and scripts
that are more illegible than the spondees of wind
that take by surprise lovers in their crypt
eyes of sand ! I am the blind force behind
the following day and the undressed ingot of gold
spur and chisel that shape marble into statues
the very noon of passion and death !

03-29-20

THE RUINS OF PHILOLOGY

if I were to write no more than this one inch
of fury and tenderness the banks of the Phlegethon
overflowing and the trills and stamps of the 7th heaven
a devastation of half begun letters and essence
of thought in disarray if I were to be known
for nothing more than this half hour of pre-dawn scribbling
this manic presumption to record an iota of the
reflections of an octogenarian living out death threats
and the entire choir of absentee bards and rishis
blinded by the unsurpassed black sun of
an inevitable noon populated by a host
of mutilated statues if I were if I were able
if only to recall the small moment in the summer of youth
when I thought the world was a capacity and
mountains were weightless minds ready to fly
if were able and I am not but remember the losses
of soul and body and the piano lessons in the grass
and the grieving suddenly tantamount to the great
echelon of disarmed angels floundering in the welkin

if I but I am not and the siegeworks of history
recorded in a series of senseless chronologies
dates and kings and saviors rank and file
driving their own automobiles down the freeway
to inferno if I were and am no more and the sequences
of lottery and myth the genealogies of gods
like shopping lists with unfounded data
regarding their armor and skin and hair all a part
of a broken epic that it took no more than a few
minutes to transcribe and the translations from
undiscovered tongues the vowel and cant
of philologists half buried in the dust of Aquinas
or Aristotle the dialogue of mayhem and retribution
the considerations of ideal and circularity
hovering in the bruited nonsense of pre-socratics
and the impossibilities of chain-letters and fugues
the alphabetic heights to ascend if but could
in order to survey the wrecks of bottomless seas
and the small pitted skin of earth and the jungles
where consonants are deployed like small weapons
brimming with poison and fire if all this
were but a half-remembered dream a nightmare
with horns and Persian glyphs and bong bong !
the evidence is not there the last and lost rhymes
the shot scattered epistemologies of Jesus
of Mahavira like a plague of running sand in the eye
if I were but am not the oracle and interpretation
of manuscript and palm-leaf inscription
cryptograms of the effusions of the dead wandering
in their Homeric capsules bleating and sorrowing
for the escaped light of their final misgivings
a literature of symbol and decapitation a single
pronouncement that all is illusion that whatever
has happened may be nothing but rock fragment
fossil and decibel of an archaic holocaust
Big Bang and quantum theory of the illustration
of the stairway to Paradise in mirror-script
upside and hopelessly entangled in Ariadne's thread
if I were but the person I used to be and not
this figment poised in a glassy reflection
waiting for one more sunrise for the horses
of the equator to run the course around the world
even before the ink has dried and the blank

page and its surrogates the asterisks that dot
the plummeting sky and all else is yes
and no more if I but and were and able

03-30-20

WHAT IS LITERATURE ?

that divine dream is speaking in the likeness
of four-armed Kali and bristling serpent speech
inaudible but for the newly dead and the curtain
of leaf and dewy mist and Dawn herself bedridden
haruspex and avenger shimmering like a dagger
in the illustrated edition and with diphthongs
painted red and the heavy tonic accent
twelve feet of meter and a pentagram to the side
ominous wheels of discourse gryphons and tedium
warlocks of interlinear translations fusion
and diction for as much as the Olympians quake
it has all been for naught a show of idioms
at the expense of pure language as practiced
in the oracular streams of Pegasus and for once
it comes down as a debacle you-for-me dialogue
that goes nowhere ego-driven mantic suffixes
can a hand stutter so eloquently ?
can an ear so fill with stone that sleeps ?
what is a cliff and a paper clip if not stop
gaps to reason the riddled pitter patter of
neo-platonic phonetic error the immense lies
finally of German didactics pressed into lunar shifts
reddening at the rim of the Wheel of the dharma
ice-caps ! Amazonian hemispherical blazes !
everything ends no sooner does the finger
set its blindspot on parchment and stains spread
the oriental hierophant babbling in his cups
comparisons between Rumi and Goethe make
no sense at all in the bamboo cluttered floors
of Magadha where the women draw circles with rice
and chafe at the long armless nights of abandon
Krishna ! hovels of desire and panting and dance
look ! look again ! the sky has no foundation
and pinkish clouds wrap their night-sweats around
the fickle waist of Lakshmi whose drum is the drone

of the infinite but unknown Number adumbrating
in the noosphere tiny alpha particles of echo
how mythical this graven image on the Neckar
floating as it does face down in a hierarchy of ripples
the transcendent nature of the spoken word !
listen ! it is nowhere only the haunted gem
coruscating on its broken planet of ampersands
life as it used to be ! lecture series on the Nymphs
whose glance is death and whose hair is the Net
of Indra ensnaring by the ankles great heroes
horses and elephants alike and the Tortoise
at the end of the grimoire and the *predictions !*
dialect continuum of the Roland cycle
horn-play and fugue and master staccato
music when it becomes poetry ! long hours
in vertigo mistaking everybody for everybody else
cinema and kabuki in the Berlitz aerodrome
spent roses and sand-clocks that have run out
time the great darkening !

03-30-20

DIANA'S HORN-CALL

what takes the sleeping stone by surprise
if not the captured ear in its distant echo
brassy memories streak the dawning sky
as it spreads its French lyric over the wood
and sounds of scampering feet faun or satyr
nymph chased by centaur the whole panoply
of arcadian verse not the least the strictures
on vowel and syllabic count and the remote
threat of thunder like a disease rippling
through the wards of melancholy and loss
and no words to explain or display grief
in its mountain of western porphyry nor
assail the imagination with cities heralded
in glass and waning lotus hues the cry !
that passes through the centuries like an
argent blade the size and shape of a crescent
moon and lunacy that abides in the unfurled
content of its doubled consonants and loud if
if were possible the recitation of the names

of the recent dead and the leafy bower and
grotto deep where lachrymose hamadryads
await the morning song hidden in branches
torn for the beauty of their haunted voices
what ! the revelry of a springtime night
the varied patterns of green in number more
than eighty four and the countless shifts of
light as it strains its awning across pools
darkening with a sylvan prescience bent
so much ! and all for naught the silvery
accent the parenthesis of blanks and gods
whose empire consists of smoke and missing
stairwells and the steep divide between what
has never been from what can never be and
yet in that horn-call the vestiges of silence
mists and fogs that peel the rocky plains
and plunge into the ampersands of sleep
gifts of a tiny summer when wrapped in
the flaring robes of diapason and flight
a world there was ! a literature of archaic
sentences riddled in the passing sands
trees and nightingales histories unbound
of hands and shields and more distant
yet the music of a marble sepulcher

03-31-20

THE FALCON : A BALLAD

I would a falcon be circling the blue unknown
a child to have never been at play with earth's
painted screens // a stone a rock cast on roiling waters
a depth of shadows lengthening the mountain's ink
a stain on the moon's waning face a faint disdain
for light and the anchors of the traveling stars
can life be measured in only forty syllables ?
and how many are the words that ply the inch
that precedes death and the plate-glass windows
where we see passing figures that resemble us
I would in the falcon's eye a day-flower yellow be
a seminary of vowels in brilliant hues of mercury
scattered pollen borne by the winds to flame
a section of the hour it takes a wing to form

and to fly from night into the grieving antipodes
a missile of mental activity a droning fly azure
with the buzz of intellectual schemes and sighs
polycephalic dreams archaic consonants buried
in the clepsydra's waist a fiction to have lingered
like a mortal on this planet's burning rim a loud
and inconsequential poem found in the vacant arm
of a deity whose whim is to carry thoughts away
fiercest cliff of residency on this troubled isle
a wight in full catastrophe of what he knows
and cannot reconcile the varied and shattered
oracle that divides itself repeatedly before
surrendering to the meaningless *ideal*
and what and more and longing and loss and
the details of air each feather has to undertake
a child to have never been a hand a shoulder
in disguise and cathedrals of envy that abound
each time a man takes a further step and lamps
that wheel around in the absent myth of sky
so many are the clustering fireflies of doubt
the immensities of sleep the drowned ignition
and the motor so heavy it cannot keep and
gravity itself the threnody of spatial error
alas a falcon I could never be but the child
spent in his toys and make-believe a foundling
in the grasses that darken each eventide
a memory perhaps and no more of the time
when you could cross a kingdom in a day

04-01-20

HEALED!

healing! healing! what's the good
for feeling so good again
turn off the lights call out the savior's
name if you can remember it
borrow an oar to row the canoe
across the Sea-of-Being and
when you reach the other shore
look around look back pinch yourself
heal! you might shout
or I been healed! better yet

and look at all the kids lying
dead on their sunday school grass
and look at all them damn fool angels
trying to repair their wings
alas! to heal or not to heal
'tis better to have drowned in glass
the reflections of the timid world
the shouts and lies of our dictators
the steady march of influenza
across the spanish Cordillera
the unwholesome retrograde
of a cinema of despair
but healed! good lord in heaven
I been healed just one more
time again and now let me
die alone in this windswept dream
remembering your once warm arms
the fondle of a day in earthly light
and gone I am forever
healed

04-01-20

THE DISCORDANT LYRE

how many the passings we have seen
and as if these streaks had never been
shapes of lightning or thunder blooming
in the keys and slips of water graceful
for their floral phrase and just as soon
vanished beneath the shade a dragonfly
poised for all eternity with vitreous wings
and skies redundant in their puzzled azure
that never seem to move owned by a
grammar of distant stone and mist
and much more have we anguished over
houses suddenly empty and missing echoes
a fabric of air shimmering and staccato
a density of ink in its fossil shape and size
the legends of music arising in grasses
that oblique patterns of vowels surround
and winds that involve the slender reed
with notes by twos and threes resounding

faintly in the sea-shell's faded gender
feminine by day and infinity by night
these passages of shadow-forms these
longings to have been hand and mind
and clouds that presume to sleep in
statues yet to be sculpted by a god
whose unknown face reverberates on high
the enormous battles of string and plectrum
the insane contest between moon and dark
the rigidities of a drop of blood against
the blackest noon-time sun the tender
shoots that wriggle to be born *again*
what does it mean to enter the *word*
of the Buddha ?
lotus petals parting at break of dawn
when blue turns to red
and red suffers the end of time

04-02-20

AN ODE IN THE TIME OF PLAGUE

our common fate to suffer a blow
from a hidden consonant a rushing
in the ear that has lapsed back into stone
a single breath in and out before moon-fall
the note struck beyond the sonic belt
and the bright coronas vibrating between
vowel and vowel in silent sacrifice
who's to know which is which among
the rife and roiling darknesses of time ?
did a hand offer to shape its syllable
unbeknownst to the fading grass ?
eventide and distant dawn and frosts
that array their sybilline elegance on
mountain peaks longing for their goddess
a round of soliloquys between knee
and burning shoulder-blade and hosts of
benighted warriors astride dun-colored hills
dead donkeys and shields split in two
by a midnight curse and dreams that ravens
are on the window sill imitating human
speech cavorting with clipped wings

and sounding the clarion of a black sun
about to rise like a mantra of spit and
contumely and still the rhymesters loud
their shouting pentameters declaim high
the absent syntax of our present tense
rock fragment and dripping stiletto
and feet discarded by philologists
stoned searching for an archaic prosody
a will to survive in the falling tone and
waterfalls crystalline as the pluperfect
heavens displayed on tents of Chinese silk
a legend in the precious stone like eyes
of haunted leopards that ravage alone
the labyrinthine cave of thread and gong
how remote the first sentence uttered
by the oracle and the island that floats
forever beyond the doubting fogs of ire
will you but fix my sleeve before I speak
and roll up the cuffs to clear my throat
and listen quick to the things I say
for never more will I them repeat
and so denying the delinquent stage
the bard unrolls his dusky parchment
and for hours that no one really counts
recites the myth of Orpheus who
invented first music then the song
in interrupted periods of mortal voice
caught in between the descant and
the irrevocable echo of punctuated silence
the drone and wasp of unheard notes
how beautiful the reverie ! alive once
and now nothing but shadowy memory
the rock and leaf the burdened firefly
alas alone the breath of exiled stars
high in the scribbled empyrean of
a far off unremembered tragedy

04-02-20

THE TROUBADOUR'S LAMENT

the rock upon which standing the word
the shred and shards of its lyric all sun
and burst of spring noontimes the bush
and the white eglantine budding on its rim
the horse of distance and the power of dust
blanching the sky's vast azure vault
and voices great and small torn from leaves
and birds above half-hidden back and forth
in their neo-latin song the chants in ivory
the rebec and vielle resounding in bazaars
where hearts search for lovers so remote
and seas and wars and mountains sudden
and strange the purpling shadows cross
the western plains and rivers flooded with
dialect and ire washing bridges away
of stone and riddled plaint soon drowned
in the womb of waters in long afternoons
and by these river-banks come memories
faint and melancholy like books that have
lost their rippling tongue and gravel-beds and
speech now foreign and filled with gaps
hiatus of the middle vowel and depths
unkenned that puzzle the darkened ear
what's to understand about this crusade ?
the foam and soot the rusting desert moon
that hangs above the lily-crested night
and horizons once youthful of delight
the syllables so clear and strict wasted
in their decay and pages fulminant
the fiery end declare and alas we souls
below who roam this enigmatic wood
born and bred in ignorant desires afloat
encompass nothing in our unmeasured span
no hand can reach no finger in its grass
can learn to recite by rote the litany
of twilights in time's crumbling ruins
still we circle endlessly the brown citadel
with a music of plaintive schemes and loss
the ivy and the rose the cheek by briars
scarred the moaning cicatrix of silence
this dream of phantom echoes tossed

04-04-20

SLEEP, ALL ELSE IS OBLIVION

the origin of things in pools of ink
obliterates the informing bright
the spreading stain across skies
once sighted through the needle
of an eye and glorious the rays
of day the hours one by one that
passed within a blink and sections
of air and clouds fulminating loud
when least occurred childhood's
brief lawn and bush and hive
how rampant bees in their nets
of desire and hues of yellow dye
and swishing in the absent ear
seas of archaic vowels weaving
spume amid albescent anchors
hands of shipwrecked dreamers
groping for the sheaves of light
until dense sleep from its corridors
descends to the soul's unknown
depths and gathers in its oval
the wandering consonants of life
'tis not this day nor the next we
ever understand to be the last but
one we hold so dear to the breast
and when not looking escapes like
jets of gas into the atmosphere
ghosts return to inhabit mirrors
long stretches of sand and distance
their hands multiply in the dark
a gleam a subterfuge of lamps as
glittering fireflies flood the screen
tiny syllables ring their silent notes
a hinge undone a door divided by
its reversal and shouts in leaves
the dance of memory as it goes
out fringe by fringe unraveled and
sleep the darkest sun consumes
all else yes all else is oblivion

04-05-20

THE APOCALYPSE TODAY

what moves and what stays still is illusory
just as the rising sun and the vanished stars
or the halcyon moon and the restless seas
and the mountains shorn of wings and grass
hibernating in a lost season and more and more
the voices cries and shivering hands the
masks of faces without identity the freeze
on thought the dwindling resource of oxygen
the catastrophic day without its noon and
up country the ghosts of horses and battle-shouts
the slogging foot soldiers gone totally astray
fingers of doubt smashing intellect of pride
and children going in circles playing dead
how bright the reddest hue the clouds dashing
for cover in the western continent and shadow
forms ineluctable grief and booklets torn
from their shrubbery the leaves dismayed
whose voices are forever silenced and patterns
of sky laid over like x-ray plates and sessions
without members and body parts dispersed
who recognizes one another who forgets
to salute the passing corpse the disarray
of hair the rumbling distance of crematoria
a flame for each name erased a number
that cannot be counted the world in its warp
a fire without smoke and the gods themselves
thin entities of paper and remorse the myths
of plague and licensed nymphs and elephants
trumpeting in a foreign war caused by a throw
of the dice and so much else the apocalypse
that is today the hour and its false minutes
to pray for light to reckon the suborned night
and choice and fabric and constellations spun
from their course the map of history a mirage
in a mirror blackened by time's fleeting wing

04-06-20

IN FAR OFF PROVENCE

I'm old I know this time of life
is not the best and the world's beset
by its constant and growing woes
a semi-invalid half-knee half knuckle-
bone a spine once erect and hair the
spare rarity caught by a winter wind
what's to cheer the despairing mind
what's to catch the failing eye or
into what ear pour springtime's murmur
in far off Provence the Albigensian Crusade
proceeds with its iron cutlery forcing
death to a language and its glorious
realms a prosody of love and longing
a loss forevermore of the song of birds
in their small latin and the bees stunned
by an unforeseen season and swords
that slice the air above Carcassonne
what am I to do lifting a finger of eld
the sprigs of eglantine withered on the brow
the fierce of verses of Arnaut Daniel
the reminder that earthly sounds ring
a hollow knell when beliefs are driven
into stone and clash the reverberations
of stubborn ideologies and chase now
the horse in its black and sweating finery
the chivalrous hero a mockery of deceit
the soon to end a world snared in disease
at my window the grayness a pallor
of all the times consumed and clouds
the brief and litany of remote skies
a remembrance that once Ovid ruled
and the chaste demurs of wet nymphs
metamorphosed into insect clans and smoke
what have I come to meditating thus
the dialect of Mistral and Aubanel
a powdery flare of yellow pollens
on the Rhone's meandering banks
and adolescent reveries of troubadours
escaped from high school libraries
the whole gamut of romance shining
in the once and only sun of Languedoc

farewell I say to those burnt at the pyre
whose credences divided good and evil
strong and in mountain-sides of grief
earth surrendered its last innocence

04-06-20

MEIN JUNGES LEBEN HAT EIN END

> "Hello Mary Lou
> Goodbye heart
> Sweet Mary Lou
> I'm so in love with you"
>   Ricky Nelson

> "They say that goin' steady is not the proper thing"
>   Elvis Presley (Wear my ring)

the preposterous number of years
since the first cyclone to hit the heart
gone by gone forever beyond count
the innumerable oblivions sectioned off
by zigzagging road trips in memory's
incunabula and what the hell get it out
the world's a pit an oyster shell tossed
in the ditch of turpitude and slander
innocence had its one and only Big Bang
when the trees shed their thousand leaves
in a single day of ocher and fading red
and a winter sky of dazzling frozen diamonds
spread its awning across snowy Minnesota hills
you can't go there again kissing in
the shadows behind mutilated auto parts
in alleys where night stays until noon
when the next day is a motel in sad neon
a thrilling ride in perfume and sprigs
of lilac and dancing in the dark
the sudden bursts of summer in corn fields
lazy meandering strolls between sheathes
of heat and opalescent shimmers
how is it we come to this age ?
unrelenting hurtled by an invisible fist
out of a high school yearbook into scraps
of eternity obituary notices and suggestions

that all will never be as it was again
ghosts with combs and eau de cologne
a ballet of swooning egrets and plumes
feathery waving whispers embraced
in repetitions of undying love
a portion of time left behind the door
and the exhaust of stars dead now more
than five thousand light years away
    Mary Lou Willard r.i.p.

04-07-20

POMP AND CIRCUMSTANCE BLUES

i

in the beginning the photographs reveal
we were all already dead precisely delineated
hair-piece and smile eyes focused
on some bogus version of eternity
motors outside gunning to take us for a ride
across the gravel extensions of time
joy-wheels spasms of intoxication and
whoops of ethereal laughter the gods
in their circumspect cruelty dressed as
rag-pickers or alcoholic tramps waiting
outside the greek Restaurants of Broadway
flirting with gasoline effigies of romance
girls doing cartwheels cheerleaders
at the Friday night football game a host
of insects with human voices buzzing around
stage lights performing HMS Pinafore
sweet little buttercup while the Photographer
with his immense swept back pompadour wig
a lesson in deceit and smooth-talk
there it was the infernal infinite design
to be born rapt with mirrors of self
and dressed and gowned and parading
with graduation diplomas and lies
about the future's immense machinery
the whole et cetera of existence mapped
on a high-wire act of atomic fission
and personality denial the eventuality
of growing up caring for a lawn and retiring

before the year is up and crowns bright
and glistening that fit the shadow head
nodding off like a silhouette against the wall
chromatic fantasy weaving the finger
of grassy fate through the mind's rachitic
opus and it all comes out as predicted
each of us already dead reciting pompous
verse and Latin epithalamia and the least
of us unrecognizable stepping out
of the photo gallery and marching into
the blaze of an enormous black sun
Pomp and Circumstance

ii

names and more names the dead stepping
two by two up and down an invisible world
props held up by the naked winds of time
salt-peter and sulfur clouds and vapors
stain the photographic essences sublime
angelic hosts for a moment hover wingless
in the late spring air and tulips and lilac
the fragrances that multiply love's rhyme
who will be the first to claim death's
wailing mouth harp and endless blues ?
Pomp and Circumstance

04-07-20

ONE DAY LESS

each day passing is a diminishment
a memory whittled or postponed
a restaurant in disguise the mortuary
the field trip to the hill-sides with
kids playing ring-around-the-rosy
all fall *dead* in somber glee and
what of the football players and
cheerleaders' pom-poms and darkness
that comes swiftly to take them by
the knees and topple the living
grace of their gymnastic forms
and what of breath turned to icicles
and the virgin Mary's weeping shoulders

mysteries of the empty cathedral
lit by a thousand votary candles
who enters never returns unless
as a rhyme scheme in Dante's poem
each day is the diminished echo
of the day before the necrology
of life's supreme moments a car
veiled in black crepe and horses
that bear the corpse of noon on
their summering backs and what !
the small faces dwindled behind masks
white budding flowers on branches
doomed for the refuse heap and
noises and rumors from *Underneath*
where Persephone sobs in her sleeves
enigma of the unfinished myth
winds that vie for etymologies
to justify their rippling shapes
that uproot in a trice the tree-of-life
and revolve the ancient seas
around a burning stellar axle
each day a day less than before
passage of vitreous reflections
quadrant of lost directions
the apex of the thought of *ending*
when there is nowhere to turn
and the hours seem like elastic
yawning through infinite afternoons
there is no primer or guide
to this grammar of foreclosure
mortals bereft of vowel and ampersand
and lexica of skies and clouds
then night and only night is
the thing that counts when days
can no longer be diminished
the little grass and the lesser leaf
the stone and its hidden flame
and fingers that have lost their hands
in the tumultuous content of air
and the myriad conclusions
that puzzle the aching mind

04-08-20

SCHOOL-DAYS : A BALLAD

wake up sleepy-head !
it's time to go to school
so what if you've lost your girlfriend
it's nature's golden rule to lose
and weep and see the light again
here's your pencil here's your
blue-lined notebook and
all your crabbed little scribbles
that amount to the daily poem
get up sleepy-head !
she's gone what's to say ?
look between the cracks
it's dawn again your Latin's
on the rise and Homer's round
the bend singing his blues again
and look at the dusty window
and out to the spreading lawn
come on sleepy-head !
life's lessons are crinkled in the grass
and the dew keeps spelling
your girl friend's lost name
a flame a smoke without fire
her memory lingers on
but sleeping more does no good
dreams are busted chased
down the drain wasted light
the flaring day's novelty
clouds where you can hide
your geometry and algebra
it's time to get a move sleepy-head !
springtime's here at last
all hue and cry luscious red
dying the air with tears
but green so green come and look
on your feet sleepy-head !
she's gone won't be back again
no more to dance with her
under the moon's painted trellis
and sing the vatic vowels
of pyramid and marketplace
get the sand out of your eyes sleepy-head !

the world's unraveled knitting
and its roar of diesel trucks
down highways you've never sped
and now the orient too is high
with its fluted azure skies
for you to reach and touch
and learn too soon to die

04-08-20

SURVIVING THE DEAD

i

in the terrific cycle of events called light
and the fragility you talked about going
through the random charts of memory
if there were something like echolalia in death
a support to the burden of oblivion the chase
down the road that leads to Hades the actors
the ones dressed like Achilles with plumes
the helmet coruscating in the late sun
if this were the last detail but for the leaves
murmuring their small grammar lessons
I lay there beside you in a false summer
afternoon with the distance of bees in our ears
turning to one another the masks came apart
I know now that was the instant we both died
though I am still a partaker of the *moly*
you remain somehow buried a victim of some
undetermined finger weighing a blade of grass
how many evenings have come full circle ?

ii

separation angst just a brief dip in the Acheron
slipping the oars into the lethal waters and
turning back to wave just once more to no one
it was like that in the photograph or the way
the lilacs bloomed at night iridescent white
and the dance and the spray attached to the wrist
and the music coming from somewhere beyond
the cornfields the circular heat of the moment
of delivery and darkness each the other held

in the suspense of a future out of balance
did we ever mature in the cross-section
of years aggravation and mold and despair ?
the unexpected was always there sorrow that
can never be learned well enough to overcome

iii

none ever come out of it *alive*
synthesis of breath and myth the overbearing
to read misunderstand and confound the letters
squiggles and folds within the eyelid
and the yellow light burdening the horizon
and the sections of air painted in all the hues
of a radiant but non-existent deity and
to firmly believe this is the first step
of immortality and all around like sheaves
waiting to be bound memories of the lifeless
who we thought would accompany us forever

04-09-20

IN PRAISE OF NOTHING

horses with war-whispers in their ears
bring noon to a complete stop parti-colored
with gold-flowered garlands and manes the
color of earth and ready to canter into battle
like in all epic poems the whinny and career
of the sounding hooves and drawing air
back and forth and the winds that drive down
from unseen mountains and the waters afar
at the very edge of the page where they are
illustrated with polysyllabic compound nouns
and adjectives and the vowels filtered between
bridle and reins and not to speak of the warriors
made of cast iron a thousand strong on one
flank and tottering toward cliff's edge and
the dozen and thirty three deities hovering
above the saffron colored dust clouds
as always poetry arises from this distant
battle-scene painted across the oriental skies
dubious recognition of virtue and muscle
and heroes designated for their tragic mien

tossed from dream to dream and idealized
in vatic and enigmatic verses and the finger
that moves out of inky night to scrawl the echoing
reverberations of their unkempt thoughts
non-linear and vibrating in the caustic sunset
how much and how dear are these capacities
of death and struggle and the virulent noises
that unsettle sleep's deepest chambers and
none to return and the stone and the plaster
and the verdant luxuries of youth destroyed
with a single carefully aimed spear and
rearing on hind legs and in a mortal sweat
their noble chargers fling off the cadavers
from their backs and plunge like nightmares
into the roiling shore waters unlit by any moon
the profound watery depths tempestuous and
such is the memory of it that blind singers
cross the wasted hills reciting the lists of names
the tumult and the tragedy of life summoned
by wild fates to involve one and all in the chase
around the ineluctable unit of mind to encompass
the tender leaf the broken twig and grass
trampled and blood-mingled bone and eye
these many and youthful saplings strong
sacrificed and sent as shadows to the Mansion
where Pluto holds forth with his stolen prize
Persephone whose mouth is sweeter than the berry

04-10-20

THE VOYAGE WITH CHARON

surprised when we heard the name of the boat
we boarded it anyway a crowd muffled strangers
some with bent crook others cowled and hooded
evasive of eye and taciturn of lip the whispers
were legend like mountains barely perceived
and lisping the waters at the sides and plunging
the splash of oars almost silent the foggy airs
musty and drift of cigarette smoke or whiffs
of alcohol from stolen flasks hands reaching
everywhere but touching nothing but shadow
no vowel was so stringent nor consonant so

dense as to disguise the meaning of any word
uttered in the motley herd we comprised
could it be the Latin poet had been correct when
he sent us hither all hexameter and oracle
the shafts of lambent late afternoon sun now
an echo of light and motionless the leaves on
either bank and the eerie ululation of the Sibyl
cramped in her verdigris bottle the rust of memory
dappling the atmosphere
so it spoke the versifier in his sleeping depths
a cormorant flew slowly in the above of time
temperature dropped ice floes and distances
ignorance really as to the nature of the universe
a collective remembrance of cities dotting
the beautiful amber colored hills of Anatolia
or just a lie that portals walls and mansions
had ever been erected on the rocky climb
uphill toward the serenity of the Temples
and they took their seats with calm countenance
the body no longer a weight to be wearied
waiting as the bark plowed through sluggish
shoals the burden of oblivion became lighter
the transformations long dictated by the god
seeming to take place as hands shook disrobing
from clammy shoulders the archaic rag all
threadbare and bone seemed to gleam and
unconsciousness in its dusky luster
what ! the ends of phrases cluttered the ear
like ingrown hairs and bunches of bees released
from frozen hives and the whir of machines
from somewhere far below and the grinding out
of stars to pepper oncoming night like fireflies
stammering fingers trying to articulate the speech
of statues and the enormous marble forms that
suddenly arose from the turgid waves
if the other shore was ever reached if the syllables
going on and on in a monotonous cacophony
a waxen syntax engraved momentarily in the mind
who would ever know to tell ?

04-10-20

THE THRONE OF THE GODS

with a white rainbow at one end of it
and a mountain of pure alcohol at the other
the world once the Throne of the gods
a relic of polluted space and out of breath
the hills we scaled as youth the woods and
crannies and swift flowing streams the air
itself invisible and royal the source of myth
ancient we have become before our time
unable to total up our losses the bereaved
and beloved whose names taken all together
spell *infinity* and how small we are in memory
boys and girls rippling in plate-glass reflections
an afternoon in a would-be paradise a bounty
of light and circular ringing of bells and
the caparisoned imagination of history as
a folk-tale relevant only in the evenings
when the mind in its opaque labyrinth recalls
titles of great Masters whose denial of reality
whose implicit sacrifice of the self whose
statuary of incomplete thoughts litters
the by-paths long forgotten by the Machine
progress and the covert menace to destroy
even as today inside our darkening capsules
we gaze out the windows matching despair
with the hour of necessity the wrist-watch
and portfolio of insurance promises ready
to burn and the sadness of all that comes
into view the bric-a-brac cities in isolation
the oceans strangled on plastic refuse
the holocaust of mankind in fossil fuels
the race to Mars ! will we ever return to
the Throne of the gods to the Olympian lies
threaded with gold and moon-luster and depths
of consciousness where beauty unravels its poetry
with sounds and syllables of ineffable echoes
the finger of clouds that descends to devastate
thunder of the occult ! boom boom in the ear
strangers come to the edge and just disappear !
it's over ! and one last thing
the *child* who came and went as we watched
helplessly the shadow and its leaf devour him

04-11-20

APRIL THE CRUELEST MONTH

lament the lessons of the willow the leafy
threnody hanging over the absent lawn
no prize for the fleeing skies nor the race
for breathing on the moon no mountain
luster shine the opaque residency on earth
the blackened distance the flagrant idioms
of despair to wit the series of vowels that
compose the echoing twilight shout and
kick the can down the road wait silently
for the rains to wash away the atlas from
its roots colored maps and hydraulic drills
phantom gods weeping over their big mistake
errant as we are straggling through the wood
a slight of hand the clouds immersed in tears
hollow booming of thunder greener than
the ichor of the forlorn deities and sing
no more the loudest grass verdant summers
passed in smothering cycles of white heat
cricket serenade hummingbird ovation
the wind the leaf the stone out of place
the west where the east can no longer be
and southland the hive where the dead
mourn the dead in a season of pure north
call down the floes of the celestial Ganges
summon to the portals of light dark Vishnu
celebrate in the tremors of the eye the lamp
whose distant passage completes a *cycle*
the last ever of that black lord the sun

04-11-20

THE ORACLE

i

we saw it once
now it's gone
curtain's up
red dust clouds
a severed head
memory

ii

what colors thought
what lessens space
what is the dark
that embraces us
even as we falter
moving through
the obscure wood
it has no answer
it is a vowel and
its unheard echo
the last time we listened
was night-fall
footsteps
no one was there

iii

a question is where
we have been and not
going anywhere else
nor stopping to consider
which day it really is
when news arrives
about the latest death
the demise of light
if we could go back
just once to the source
a bright ribbon circling
the air we breathe
the voices of leaves
bringing distance
to our ears

iv

we will leave it alone
as there is no way
we can move the past

04-12-20

MEDITATION

or as in ancient India with its flooded river plains
on each mountain peak some god or other
adjusting his tiger skin or reducing to ashes
with a baleful glare anyone who opposes—
such distances and mantras and droning skies
naked seers blinded by a blackened noon-day light
orating on the loss of focus on the need for nothing
burying the caustic ego in a cacophony of chants
syllables rotating like points of light and sudden
illuminations cross-legged seated beneath a holy leaf
no self they cry burning with austerities matted
locks brides nine days old and the fire *within*
and what of us some three thousand or a million
kalpas hence denizens of some dense and dreaded
kaliyuga unable to distinguish Krishna from Buddha
lambent spikes of flame the mind confound and
athirst for the knowledge that will eliminate
salvation what about *that* ? separate the colors
red black green and white and what of yellow
or ocher the fustian dull of burnt hillsides and
the tapestry of braided cities spoiling landscapes
fumigated airs and enigmatic rutilating voices
loud with consonant clusters that mar the clouds
as they race from thunder to thunder in the vast
theater of space and what of us these countless eons
into the future confusing psychoanalysis for
simplicity of the dharma as preached in old Magadha
still baffled by inherent sorrow and desire and
what to do about the world condition whether
to sow a new mutation or let alone the ancient rice
in its oriental beds of sleep and what of us these
nine million dozen centuries of hectic re-written
histories the elimination of doubt and the turning
of the Wheel and the spit that dries in our fevered

mouths and the recitations of spells and formulae
meant to keep disease at bay and the coronation
of new gods bathed in camphor and mineral oils
and what of the sixteen thousand girl-friends
of Krishna naked on the full-moon night running
without their bodies to bathe in the Yamuna
a chrysalis of sanctity in their breathless rush
for each one is the re-birth of a Vedic stanza and
what about us puzzled at the meaning of each sound
emitted by the earth-destroyer Shiva on his manic
cycles of love and resurrection wedded to Uma
whose swaying elephant gait makes the planet tremble
can't we see this is the end of the countless trillion ends ?
it was all foreseen and hidden in the unchewed leaf
of the holy Tulsi plant but for us the passing whirl
of events is but a lightning bolt a break in the empire
of Light and confusion is our daily fare and plunder
and mutiny and political platforms built on rust
must we pray for the silence that follows destruction
of the cosmos plaiting and weaving our fornicating thoughts
in temple-plans tangled in the jungles of Tamil-Nad ?
away with the body of the mind ! let us then drown
the shadow in these pools of jade and twilight
alone each and every one as the pronouns we employed
serve no other purpose than to divide
and immerse ourselves in the passage that follows death
like bright-winged moths or fireflies imagined
just once in the far distant brain of the Archetype
asleep forever in a bed of unconscious stone

04-12-20

OMBRE D'INFERNO

aprite ! aprite ! tenebrose porte !
from behind the red curtain the shaking
shivers of envy as the world ever at odds
with itself the world pivoting like a small dot
on the tip of a spear aimed at the breast-plate
of Achilles and the smaller ones whose minds
are not at rest and for whom the rains and leaves
that abound in them and the echoes of grasses
and the trees budding with cherry and plum blossoms
and from behind the black curtain the whoops
and wailing the ones who missed the traffic
heading for Northfield MN and the buses
half in flame half without smoke plunging
through darkness and the chaos of the stars
ballet of the ungrateful they call it and clouds
the shape of human emotions and thundering
silently in the morass of distance and the lesser
ones whose billets and pikes are useless
and whose hands remain fixed with questions
about the other life the redundancies of breath
existence on the edge shoulders aching with grief
the stone weights that measure the illusions
created in the eye as it scours the horizon
for earth the dimensions and widths of which
who can tell ? why the importance of knowledge
the affirmation of light the mirages on the highway
heading for Northfield MN on a cold winter night
where the dormitories are peopled with the dead
and the college courses offer no salvation
no relief from the apparent and impending
end the so-called diversion from the mountain's
western slopes where madness and the still point
of the mind as it verges on its milestone of thought
perception and abstract of plenitude crowded
with historical untruths the lies of biology
and trigonometry in text books colored with sand
and from behind the green curtain the children
who asked not to be born whose precincts
of plastic toys and cellophane wrapped chocolates
the fuming et cetera of the smallest pleasures
inanities of sky and tribulation the shadows

rising from some infernal horizon coming
to take back their echoes and finger-tips
the edge of confusion and doorways that open
only inwards so there is no escape and the speech
and folio of those behind the yellow and last curtain
who lacked the money to buy tickets to go
to Northfield MN and missed the party and
the pom-poms and wrist-bouquets and halcyon
instructions to dance with ghosts *our* ghosts
and the drum and conch resounding deep into sleep
not to wake again only the eiderdown of death
beneath the rock and silhouette a song at best
haunting ricocheting into the ear's unfathomable
depths of inverted pyramid and ash
the cavernous voice of Pluto

04-13-20

A GLIMPSE OF THE GODDESS

milk white sheen of her brow
resplendent in the dense night
arms like peninsulas of sleep
reaching out to embrace atmospheres
where the dwindling mortal fates
dream there is substance to time
hair and its massive miles of ink
locks that dangle coyly unkempt
covering one eye the other wide
with surprise at the relief of mountains
gales and whispers of summer tempests
her hands that cup the wild seas
to drink of the lees and drunk
step into the abyss of perpetuity
her *peplos* torn at the hem
her knees the distance between
two infinities and nothing
how she steps dancing clouds
fanciful aerobatics with the color red
ankles and feet of pure alabaster
delicacies of the myth of no-return
at her ears the ship of echo
yearning to arrive at its source

shells and cowrie beads and gleams
of the moon caught in her phase
of becoming and disappearing
hours that wrap like bracelets
her pivoting wrists and fingers !
rings too many to count that shine
multi-hued in the face of death
passing as she does eternally
through the unspoken vowels
of mind and its labyrinthine prayer
do we but think to catch
a glimpse of her as she rotates
on the alpha of imagination
inventing her steps through stone
as she chews the baleful leaf
and breathes the oracle of grass
esteem of the uncounted planets !
her earth is the garden of dew
we hold to the glass each dawn
as if she ever had a shadow to cast
or some form of boundless air

04-14-20

"THE BROKEN HARBOR OF THE SUN"

"Porque el amor dura sólo una noche!"
M.A. Asturias, Leyendas de Guatemala

warnings about the risk of immortality
and the dream of recurring love with a stranger
who lives just next door in her oriental envelope
of red ink block-print and a signature
derived from the blue lotuses that perpetuate
the fields out back and to see her once more
a gain on the austerity of wind and soil
the air cries as love's ruthless dart pierces it
what was the red piece of paper
she slipped under the door ?
it's all in a man's life a hotel room rented
for a single night bleeding and narcissi
that overwhelm the tub before dawn
the airplane's remote wing already silver
with disintegration and the calliope echoing

the ear's grief and misunderstanding of depth
enormous ocean in either Toltec or Sanskrit
deities of obsidian and palm-leaf inscribing
on their skins the ancient legends of dew and grass
speak louder please ! demands of hills for horizons
perfections of drill and flute the sorrowing
how archaic the verb that acts as an accident !
I know her ! I *knew* her ! cycle of heat
within the cloistered eye and submerged
continents in a single votive act of emergency
let it go ! fuse and fiction of the late sun
setting in its orangery behind the stone
"another hero dead" ! what's to understand ?
and dressed in nothing but a trench coat
the long braid of her puzzling hair prepared
for rain and the way she shut the door
the profile of her face like the map of Japan
as it lapsed out of the dream into the Unknown

    for Nikki Arai , again

04-15-20

INCUNABULA

the definite article and the first person pronoun
dissolve in an instant the paper they employ
how they clamor for a bed of sky for clouds
for verbs of intuition and demolition
to talk hibernating in the instamatic vowel
of disbelief the various numinous entities
on all fours and pleading for votive relief if only
a single altar one flame a few ashes mortals !
see it streaking across the heavens !
a meteorite of blazing consonants the loud
and violent premonition of the finish
its syllabic quantities of smoke and echo
how they babble in their ruminating sleep
inventing one universe after another and
jungles where language is born in glyphs of stone
and alternating rock and leaf and dew-fall
to sound out the holy fictions of the Origins
mythifying the Nymphs who dwell in pools
the length of ink and sabotage and high

the fluted hair in tresses of musical notes
that seem to summon out of the passing winds
strangers and heroes bent on battle
how can they presume against the gods ?
to wit the parchments of ineffable words
action and libel defeat and mourning
gifts of the Supreme ones the lot of mankind
gestures without meaning arms elevated
above the broad-brimmed hat of Mercury
as if to appeal to the door of justice
was it ever this way all accent and tone
nothing that can be transcribed let alone
translated in the enormous fan-leaf ?
hearing is counted by the amount of tears
defying air and its brittle constructs
of dream and infatuation and whatever else
the absence of syntax signifies in leaves
torn from the apogee of immortality
the alas and woebegone briefness of life
as one by one the oracular hues fade
from the agrammatical speech of the gods

04-15-20

DARK: THE SUBJECT OF POETRY

flowers born of thunder indigo and periwinkle
blooming where the eye returns its night
to unfathomable surfaces of sleep
what is there to see come the false dawn
attributes of color and air fiction
of light spreading weightlessly over hills
remembering the season of trees and showers
noon in the abscess of time ! a reason to forget
we were ever more than what our dreams told us
inventions of letters and water and smoke
and what of that archaic wheel of revolving lava
lit up like a chrysalis of fireflies each morning
shedding its flagons of rays and luster
over the *departing* earth ?
hours of myth ! totemic incidents in the wood
where cursed to wander without north
our shadows clumsy and shapeless knock

against vestiges of dew and leaf the briefest
of days for time shortens everything
it is already ancient this Thursday a chalk-marked
point in a sequence of disappearing relations
threatened by the *death* inherent in the vowel O
the great omega the finish of all sounds
lack of echo and stone only a vast
field spreading its shadow across perception
what's to know in this moment of conjecture
and night-fall ? a once and only abstraction
sketched in a black mirror and yearning
for hands to hold it searching for a clue
to the irreversible enigma of breath
poetry ! unfound silver restless gold
fillets of ivy around the pale brow vanishing
accolades of triumph in the contest held
on rocky crags between Pan and Apollo
who wins in the essay to define beauty ?
eglantine prize to the *troubadour*
without identity and yet impassioned
who sings the new season of verdure and Beyond
where a dark nameless lady awaits
to take him *lifeless* in her profound embrace

04-16-20

CRICKET SONG

short is brief for breath on earth
and light is once and never more
small shades have the boat sunk
like leaves dipped in a darkened pool
heights are bright above the eye
and cliffs resound with gorgeous noise
flanked by changing moons night
circles its only self and disappears
what song is played crickets make
what music in the unheard ear !
echoes of a grassy morn a field
spreading radiance left unseen
we fret the wandering chord and
sound the arrow's swift release
like bees swarming purple blooms

or hummingbird suspended in air
wings too quick flashing hues
that summer in memory's vestibule
hark ! my child hold fast no more
to patterns the mind designs
all days are one and none remain
the elastic rope of sky moves on
too fast and thunder in vast whorls
peals like brass bells in our sleep
where was here if nothing lasts
one direction suits all facing south
where the dead in their red canopy
relate each passing hour a dream
none can recall and lasting slumber
takes their hands' enfeebled prayers
and offers them to a forgotten noon
hark ! my child hold fast no more
to patterns the mind designs

04-17-20

THE CORRUPTION OF LIGHT

for Peter Ganick r.i.p.

the fuse the field the fugue the fission and fiction
of all the visible and known remain unseen to the mind
whatever illumined all three worlds whatever
gave flame to the nascent day whatever page
was turned to reveal the beginnings of script
words half-formed hues of meaning epic and echo
the vast and the panoply the armory of thought
cribbed and labyrinthine the hearth where
ideas circulate waiting to be discovered
somewhere on the Ionian shores or in the crevices
of Himalayan foothills or in remote Cathay
history revealed in one moment and in the next
annihilated by the wick and temperament of ire
the gassed tribulations brought on by envy
the animal turpitude and scorn latent in
the human endeavor and what else would you have
paragraphs and indentations and arrows
pointing to north and south simultaneously
an encyclopedia of misdirection and hybris

entire childhoods uprooted from hill-slopes
where dialects spawn chronologies of memory
the oblivions and targets whereby men barter
for conscience and the various similitudes
of metaphor and warfare and then the remainder
tossed into ditches or wholesale basements
disregarded and isolated the aesthetics of light !
a finger of grass up the spine of sky and clouds
working themselves through the elements of number
and thunder and the coruscating gravities
of alternate universes if such may be and entire
fractions of mountains winged and supernal
in the necrologies of the gods what a thing !
we go through the index cards rotating letters
of an alphabet or designations of hieroglyphs
and birth-records of heroes and their losses
grammar of the irrevocable schoolyard
if we could only ! the saying and the heard the one
plus the other *one* and the sum of each half
during the rains and the tropical origins of sound
leaf by leaf learning to articulate vowels clustered
around a diaphanous consonant at the start
of creation and yet and yet where is the lamp ?
is it only *language* by which we perceive and
draw outlines of air ? and the swart sun spinning
its dizzy horses through needles of sweat
and aloud and infantile at once the courage to speak
as statues do on the appointed day of judgment
marble and obtuse testimonies and weeping
the sorrow of parades after the battle and saints
gaunt half-naked in torn saffron rags knee and
ankle and shoulder each the envoy of grief
don't you recall that afternoon ? it was after
the telephone was invented and the funeral
we sat there in our new cloth suits loosening
our ties and contemplated the *yes* of eternity
below us a street continued to move slowly
through the burden of heat and transmigration
of souls and the bric-a-brac of poetry !
and behind us billowy and enormous *Kukulcan*
salvation of knives ! dressing up his mounds
of talking bone and evanescence with colors
indescribable looms of red and green and yellow

becoming black as music in the ear of stone
trespassing the land of the dead we were
and ignorant of how the cosmos comes to be and
ends and the corruption above all of light
between us we passed back and forth the bottle
the elixir of life the fire-water the trap !
did we not recognize who was in that coffin ?

04-18-20

IVAN AND JOE CREATING GALACTIC CITIES EMPORIA OF THE SOUL LOST SUBURBS OF THE MOON CRATERS OF THOUGHT THE ENDEAVOR TO SURVIVE

for Laurita

whatever shape or hue of paper came to hand
a map developed spawning other cities as
we huddled on the green living room rug
embracing the radio's auditory hallucinations
boulevards spiked between verdant slopes
or heading like crazy adolescents into an ocean
drizzled with piers and wharves and beach-fronts
neon signs everywhere glitter of on-and-off
which city was this Babylon Cairo or Gotham
certainly with caped super-heroes or shady
undercover cops or cowboys in blue and red
bandanas riding phantom horses of smoke
through the twisting canyons of suburban
development and the invention of metal
and putting into place pistons and gears and
the involved sky of the x-ray and sprawling
yellow with its Olympus and ready-made Zeus
whose profound and cavernous voice foretold
mysteries and enigmas of *being* even as bent over
our great designs planetary urban centers arose
formations of air and light in and around curlicue
streets climbing ivy smothered mountain-sides
and hills where new dialects and ideograms
swarmed with translations and theogonies
diversity of neighborhoods with Mexicans and

Greeks and the ill-begotten sons of doctors idle
and rich in their flivvers of quicksilver and lime
what a host of blocks and squares and circles
terraces with latitudes of Brazil or Rio Plata
and down to earth distances where dimming
flashlights turn into auto wrecks in ditches and
summer songs beside placid lakes with girlfriends
whose aching takes on the outlines of Bermuda
or some fancy Pirate island dubbed in azure
in a sea of stucco and hyaline solution and still
places where skyscrapers grow like fungi and
lurid waterfront commercial districts rampant
with crime and illicit trade and night-shade and
corruptions of lamps and jars of fireflies the mind !
what to name such an excess of metropolises ?
using a red pencil for broad thoroughfares and
green or orange crayons for country clubs or
hospitals and blue for lagoons that dot the eye
and ochre for the plenitude of schools high and
low and by the margins where the paper runs
its course the cemeteries where suns rise and set
and legends of ancestors in broad-brimmed hats
who've come from places with no logic and schemes
to build even finer cities with crenelated walls
and towers named after Arthurian knights all
in a single afternoon beside the mythic wireless
days out of time that never end : our childhood

04-18-20

"SPARKLE"

cannot bear more the connections
stuttering hands eyes and leaves
yearning focus of the unseen in sleep
dreaming it was all otherwise the
trade off in bodies and trees and
heights never to be scaled even
as Juno complains that Troy
was betrayed and walls and moats
freighted with headless trunks
of the flower of youth et cetera
the babble of epic and storm and

illusory devices that run the x-ray
and heavens in ultra-violet code
we are come to this planet hod
and mortar the divine instructions
fail to translate the roadways
fiery clouds and transmission of
alphabets from the dead down south
where trembling earths turn blue
diseased by the human clause
and whatever nature corrupted
by an invisible flame and grasses
great and tall waving and weaving
in a memory saddled by rocky
distances and the small cries
issuing from beneath the hills
wanting back the vowels of their
souls fleeting intermittences
dissolving even as they wing forth
into the sparkle of an unknown day

04-19-20

APRIL 20 TWENTY-TWENTY

at long last the day of nothing
the bloom on the glass the door
that won't open the upper floor
emptied of its satraps and dolls
footsteps on the stairway that
only go up into a silent dusk
nothing returns today it's all
a go at the passing wind the whim
of hues faded on the leaf the eye
unable to understand its own shape
circularity of the seasons and
fuse and bang of an ear gone deaf
why is it the ringing won't stop
the concrete seems to ripple
without cause as it yearns to meet
the sky at an unknown junction
appearances are not everything
stars and grass the rushing seas
prepared to empty their echoes

in the residing stone of crowns
it is the aching heart the dolorous
phantom memory of someone
who should not have gone so soon
entries to inferno multiply today
the parking lot and the bike path
woods that hold secrets of time
a page missing from the Book
calendar dates that never existed
should we want to go home today
there would be no baedekker
to guide us no library to reckon
which is the best possible poem
best off we are holding back
by the dry well and temple ruin
the hills into which we dissolve
come eventide the ruminant
moon rising over the hair-line
and distance the ever vanishing

04-20-20

CLASSICAL PHILOLOGY

can we determine the course of language
the phonetic shift from manual to casual
the vowels gone hybrid and the tonic
accent dissolved of its function in
the circle of echoes derived from the
oracular leaf a distance of syllables
each separated by a hiatus in memory
body and thought of the archaic root
the verb principle and lesser *to be*
irregularities of person and number
masks of the consonants worn over
the eyes of statues at noon the height
of pronunciation in decibels of smoke
how loud the sky crashing silently
at the end of the hour when the kids
pack up their books and chalk flinging
wild glances at the blackboard's sea
where the weary Trojan fleet drowns
were it not for Venus in her see-though

to salvage the origins of poetry in salt
weaving her sandaled feet through waves
of hexameter scanning the lines for meter
up and down macron and breath loaned
unconsciously from the Homeric pitch
and for centuries locked into this device
tumblers and tricks handiwork of gods
whose numinous qualities exist only
in the scholiasts' copious byzantine notes
files of thumb and grass epodes and epistles
skimmed by the brimming Renaissance eye
columns to the left remaining unmatched
even as the newer forms emerge dominant
the nasal orient the southern noun
the adjectives determined three ways
to accompany the dead in their droning
a hectic motley parade as they enter
the portals of Avernus waiting for
chance encounter of epic metamorphoses
Daphne on the hillside chased by the sun
and shrill the cries of Naiads in the pool
where enamored Narcissus seeks his face
the polyglot round of identities known
as philology and the heavens themselves
a grammar of distance and nostalgia
long afternoons spent in the Rumor
of hives and the swarms of insect tribes
dreaming in the drum's polished ear
where the small intaglio of sleep resumes
its etymology in unshaped Attic marble
just as we the students of Literature
grown weary pass into dialect forms
to wake in modern times corrupted
by the invention of electricity and noise
no longer able to identify the Pronoun
nor to speak in heroic stanzas
lost in ruined descriptions of the *Nymph*
in her strophes of all alluring death

04-20-20

HOW IT STANDS TODAY

serpents demons fiends thrust from the heavens
to do battle with and by the shore exultant cries
and the hollow ships echoing the clamor and
who will stay the execution and who will climb
aboard and steer the course through the reefs
rocky shoals wild surf bearing the mottled trunks
of warriors once their mothers' pride the junction
between the southern horizon and pure devastation
placing phalanx upon phalanx and the flowers
hand-held and the speechifying still ringing in the ear
echo of so many histories past and myth of fruition and
heights and benign deities if there be such smiling
through the ether while the surgeons remove waste
of thought and cunning and plying sword against
sword the din of war that reckons no number
is too high for mortality the mountains thunder
back a grief and hills shorn of their dialect mourn
and the wood and river and the nestled groves
where played nymph and legend the distant glint
were but all these come to pass and the underside
the bottomless pool the indistinct twilights and
suns blacker by the day rising and setting without
proportion or divinity and come let me tell you more
the days of high school and the pom-poms and parade
the uniforms laid out for the stage and this and that
the street names emboldened by light and plate glass
a reflection of masks portraying their opposites
an entire panoply of idioms pointing toward an egress
and Lo the shadowy fields where go those whetted
on promises of reward and afterlife and moving
as phantoms through temple ruins rock-folds
and eerie defiles come night-fall and the world in
its illusory sleep beneath a savage ruddy moon
and who can hear then the last sighs and breaths
the tented beneath canopies of dust and melancholy
amen it says everywhere in blunted song and choirs
of the archaic who dwell between the pages of the Book
somewhere in an orient of vowels and aerial signals
the leaf in its outline of silence and longing
torn from its branch and dripping quietly the dew
soon to vanish from earthly property and

04-21-20

MESSAGE IN A BOTTLE

let's face it the world as we know it is no more
the space tracker the troops amassed at the border
the Argives and Trojans no less than the armies
organized by the Kauravas and Pandavas far off
on the steamy gangetic plains and the rush to get
to Mars hub of ire and flux of the color red and
who knows what new technological device that
can bring us no nearer to the control of heat
or noxious gasses nor the positions to the left or
right of chest-thumping politicians using oratory
stolen from the Romans as we know it is no more
but fictitious devices plots on loan dialogues of
system overdrive the cliff toward which we speed
dreaming this is the Narcissus track to heaven
nay Brother this is the end of the end the exception
without cause the phrase that cannot be translated
even as we try to order the sequence of vowels
and a knight from nowhere comes galloping on
his steed of sweat and nerve black as the noon
when statues are delivered of their stasis and
as we know it is no more and lay the grasses down
and try to summon dead prophets from their nine
year sleep as if to learn the how and the why of
the this and the that and portents in the sky
at three in the morning when the airplanes have
all been grounded and the wireless signals not
kid ourselves the world as if we were drawings
in a Sunday cartoon page being turned by thumb
and grief and the solemnities of the Pope striding
solitary across the great marbles of Italian civilization
as we know it wormwood and rot psychosis and
blue litmus tests that reveal we all have *it* the disease
called man the supernal profligate devotee of progress
don't you remember the 18th century and the concerto
grosso and the epistolary novel and Prague and Venice ?
not as it used to be or was and the consonants that
bear in their wake enormous secret conflagrations
consuming whole texts of aesthetics and speculation
Nirvana ! the host of bodhisattvas swarming and
kid ourselves this is not what used to be high school
and the Broadway and Center street that marked

believe it or not the midpoint of the universe when
Joe played the tuba on Memorial Day and warriors
were checked off by stone and descant and thrilling
as it seemed fireworks on display as if to celebrate
what ! the little we seem to be clinging to our leaf
the briefest green of breath the memory of what
appeared as we lapsed in library day-dreams when
each page was a picture of animal simplicity not
what it is now the end of the world as it used to be
kid ourselves not stripe and accent and bitter tone
echoes that flute the rock formations of the mind
fading Morse code from all devouring Black Hole
dot dot dot *can you hear me ?*

04-22-20

MISSA BREVIS

qui tollis peccata mundi

the end and the beginning front and back
which of either side is the correct one
or in fact there is no center and the margins
contract and expand in waves ad infinitum
refrigerated accidents in space uncountable
and unnameable pointillistic dots surfing ink
question of circularity and lack of depth
sheer horizons bending around a fuse
for months he lay in a coma endless summer
today masks of solitary indignation
innumerable the sorrow and waste earth
its progeny shunted back and forth the lay
of archaic gods of stone and leaf born
and the skies the toil of hexameters
rolling across the knife of time and who suffers
and who shares grief with knee and shoulder
and traffic of burnt angels streaming through
the night and voices that pierce hospital walls
and when he came to it was in a different city
abandonment of the thesis of salvation
eating for want of hope and staring upwards
as if a promontory of light should at last appear
and the clothes were distributed among them
as they lay naked and shivering the denizens

and mother Gaia stepped from the vestibule
to anoint the fevered brow of each
how much wailing vowel and the attributes
of poetry and melancholy gathered in sheets
the difficulty in recognizing his surroundings
a puzzle interred in the massive silences
how is one to connect the dots and survive ?
music ! delicate counterpoint of axis and wheel
smoke issuing from the sea's gaping wound
the electric fishes of the *Fathers* desperate to breathe
memory dives inwards in a lost reflection
to winnow the plaintive grasses of twilight
shadow forms weaving through rock fragments
souls yearning in the incomplete history of leaves
everyone has been here before !
only to return to the dark intermittence

04-23-20

[FROM *THE HYMN TO GAIA*]

hoarse voice of Agamemnon bawling out some curse
as if to arouse from the seas a team of dead horses
the roiling registers of broken spear and diadem
the ancient faculties of light doused in violent spray
to condemn and to put to the test temper of Zeus
the almighty thunderhead of Olympus and angry
rebuttal of sense swift and keen the vowel-like darts
piercing to the heart fool-hardy Argives et cetera
pebbles and fractions of water and loose rolling grass
all across the western front where *night* limits the eye
and hills suddenly born from ancient earth wounds
a hand flings its quoits into the fray using a language
borrowed from sleep and rock and the dusty toil
of chariots working blindly to return the course and
sliding swiftly from view the nouns of recapitulation
each verse a fragment of echo salt and rust and brine
legendary slips in and out grottos clefts damp hideouts
of nymph and goddess torn at the knee her fringe of cloth
yellowing in the endless afternoon when words lose
all meaning the head pounded by the solitary drum of silence
a vast and eloquent myth unraveling in the cloud-work
turning ruddy with contempt and issuing swarms of

bees maddened with the odors of so much wild thyme
climbing the trellises and vines trodden by blind souls
looking for the entrance to Hades and the flowering
wonder of twilight in the mind whitening blooms
and the chaste footprint of Artemis in the soft mass
of thought the nevertheless opprobrium and gravity
each limb weighted with metal and sweat and bell-like
cavities in the ear's dark fosses yet retain nothing of
the sound of earth turning moaning as it does nightly

02-23-20

"... WITH FACES IN THE DUST"

Ajax and Ares and the non-committal gods
who unravel the scripted cities of heaven
is this a joke ? can the seas be so redundant ?
are there actually histories that have not been
written chronologies and hagiographies of rock
and the bleeding beneath the grasses and nectar
poured from the horn of memory and what of
the illusionists who are born daily and die
by nightfall the leaf and dust and ennui
that cannot be dispelled in reading the Text
of ambivalence and oblivion and what were
you doing that day when the gongs went off
and the red siren circled its own silence and
from afar the casual ones in medical garb
who probe the abscess for an answer and dark
the relative pronoun and darker still grammar
of the afternoon and where did you go afterwards
when the streets were emptied of their adjectives
and a hush settled over the grove and pool
with its boundless depths of night and masked
adventurers riding phantom steeds the panoply
of literature hailed the oncoming trees and hills
and great was the loud and supernal the hoof
immensely azure the distances between child
and flower-fold the prints being erased on glass
reflections of the puerperal mind as it enters
the ninth sphere and gravity is excised of its
spectacular vowels and down comes the *All*
and evening finds you back at the shore trying

to assemble the tent and crying and longing
dominate your senses and you listen and you
keep listening for the passage where sleep
like threads of sand enters the right ear and
you lay the head down as if it were stone and
dream you were somewhere on earth talking
as statues do to the noontime remnants of marble
looking for the source of light only to be puzzled
recalling the inky stillness with faces in the dust

04-24-20

THE SEER IN HIS CUPS

everything I see is everywhere the horizon green
the dun and sated hills I recall falling beneath twilight
so often when words only puzzle coming forth the mind
dwindles in darkness fain I would commit to sound
the tongue of grass and leaves echo the even fainter hue
that creeps into the ear if I can hear that far but only
the child of memory his death day and tribulation
the price of breath and distance haunting corridors
where ink comes to a halt and issuing from the rear
a door with virtues of invisibility and height if
and if only is a syllable and I question too the bottle
where it hides conditional and querulous so I read
picking up the molded text the verbiage of afar
the isolated and endless rhymes occur to the head
and falter like stone to understand the script
spread out like sunlight on a sheet of water thin
as the shadow it involves and heat and remote the
cavity where buried vowels of what I know distend
a peninsula of night a sequence of dots and signatures
I am among those things a ghosting of rock and glen
mistaking always the diphthong for its mire and
shooting buds the hand designs its future reverie
a painted glyph and the gloaming where quivering
outlines of the arrow speeding forth its intaglio
underscores and finally the famous smoke ascends
from where I stand and discern the cloudy field
high in the mansions of unseen sky and Lo the movie
devolves and a script of ancient cities sounding

as they do in the quire of unpaged time a music
that is the all at once and nowhere I ever was
04-24-20

SATURDAY MORNING ON THE LIBRARY STEPS

I address now and both in sorrow and grief
just as a great crag juts out among the roiling waves
and men on earth still live on insults and debt
set up kindling for offering a great ox fatted and
smoke rising to the cerulean mansions where deafened
by the drum of eternity weary gods toil at a meal
pouring wine from a fractured vase and the ether
milling around on the ragged beach where the gray
surf pounds ceaselessly into the night's ears and
asked to count just how many were left who had
embarked ten years ago pouring barley meal out
the palms of their hands raw from rowing and
what's more I will recite to you name after name
and search the library for a clue as to the source
of the water and high bound the masts creaking
ready to split like mere splinters in the angry
gusts of Aeolus out of the bag and voracious for
the deaths of you whom I espy through legends
of timber and hill and ask who will wake the sun
from his slumber who will anoint the eastern rim
who will indeed ? and chanting confused vowels
they lie down and rags and fetters both on the sand
dusky turmoil fills their dreams even as you turn
the pages before you illustrated with line drawings
of them the routed and scrappy heroes aching and
went down among them to Hades to search the nesses
for a lamp and faced the bewildered I am crying
as much as I ever have and restless to know
how the Polis will fare and the gates left ajar
and who of them are you I demand in the maze
one foot there and the other nowhere and feel pulling
at the ankle phantom hands the grist of memory
a dust pall a choking of envy and when was the meadow
the light and the newness of leaf come the rosy flare
each of them you husks of longing the defeated
emblem and signature in the air left trailing echoes
of a voice or voices yours the damned heteroclitic as

the fires left crackling by the mound where lie
the once emblazoned sons of kings princes like
leopards who once prowled the demesne a fierce lot
taxed by usurers and given a false pedigree as pride
the human morass still dunned in these unnamed halls
will I approach but one of you and say what ?!
so it is today I am older than those among you waiting
for the library to open its windows and air the fresh
and a season to begin not as begging but triumph
the many lights and breathing as once did all

04-25-20

HYMN TO THE MUSES

from whom we cull the notes that meld
with winds on high the lyric fierce that
graces branch and leaf their distant
voices sigh with raiment of echo wild
and hair flown with enchantments spread
across the distances of bounteous air
and did they not their eyes turn in to
see the pattern of the dancing mind and
give to each the other's thought woven
between the several vowels and sounding
like stone against a moving water and
gathered grasses in their summer hands
the finery of finger knuckled silently
in the round of breezes tossed like light
through the mountain of their birth
from which they take their embodiment
ethereal as the moon remote that rises
now and then to enhance the nightly
sky and stars alike their own souls bright
aglitter in the poetry of long desire
to know as they the time of life a well
hidden in the glades that know no west
and comfort take from their soothing
melodies borne by invisible consonants
to mortal ears and spires of red and
luster of lotus floating downstream in
the afternoon of childhood's infinity
yes but once hold to the breast the beat

of their eternal drum the triangle of
crystal singing the tiny bells the dew
brings at the opening of each day
would we be as much as they immortal
for an hour before turning the purple
page of the deep and sleep forever more

04-25-20

THE WORK OF POETRY

"The Mirrhe sweete bleeding in the bitter wound"
The Faerie Queene, Bk I, 1. 9

Neptune then his placid head rears above the wave
and scattered over glabrous waters the sun's heroes
to timber and plank cling and poetry ascends to view
the array of hexameter and grief the instantaneous
vision a glimpse between trees sacred to the wood
where lost and what else demeans the curve of thought
each mortal by his self a wanderer in the lees of mind
a section of air that deepens dark distress and wounds
that open like margins imagined at the edge of space
to reveal pearly white memory's fading sepulcher
stone and script the ancient syllables effaced and
as the haughty wind of rhyme resolves the leafy song
into phrases green with oracular secret and even more
the human kind itself devours with doubt and sleep
the restless engine that twines grass and twilight's dim
whatever a next day brings is never the forth of time
but a relic of temper the previous hour had declined
and setting shadow upon shadow the crystal walls
recede and hills dun and pale the expanses hide again
how can this be the only time to wake ? the aching
tongue the missing words the sentences never done
their revolving search for vowel and tone the accent
to place where spent emotion puzzles its cuprous while
such it is these minutes that round the spinning thread
and thumb and shoulder whatever else the dolorous
wheel grinds down what is this man a person or
a mask the shade of archaic reveries staged on rocky
fragments between thirst for light and dying breath
a nymph who wades out into the shoals and her hand
reaches forth but did not the trident shear the lamp

and take away the illusion of the poet in his rampant
arrogance the suits and finery of delusion's *Court*
to find the perfect note the music that rends both
present and past hurtling them from the Rotation
of the celestial gyres that gives us but brief reckoning
a remembrance of sweet paradise that never was

04-26-20

DANDELIONS

and just who are we this uncounted day
and what and where are the revolving accidents
the space between the several hours of time
allotted to our mortal illusions red and bright
in the one parenthesis we live and breathe
and in the other we choose to die and between
either one the difference is hard to tell
a book a plate a chosen bunch of grapes
some cheese the shepherd offers us a summer
repast by the shady nook and glen this
childhood we measure in a single crystal instant
a volume of air a tablet of azure shimmering pure
and waking from this mirage what we ask
and why each the other no longer recognize
and clouds that scurry scattering our minds
shadow projections in a deserted movie theater
talking we hear and sounds from another time
and horses round the bend and flames of ire
ears pricked up and nostrils flaring wild
then disappear as smoke always does from a pyre
a corpse we are become walking still among
the ruins of some Attic temple fine a sculpted
frieze our wandering thoughts fixed in marble
for all in later years to puzzle over the enigma
we had become the two once one and now
no number serves to define no cipher to defend
the pronoun we once were pale fading breath
absences among dandelions curlicues of death

04-26-20

SCHOOL-BOY

"et vera incessu patuit dea"
  Aeneid, I, 405

and I heard Hari's voice talking in a dream
all other reveries and mirages past and present
were erased by the thundering echo of his words
count no more backwards or forwards he advised
for there is no number but in the middle
and looking back I saw him disappear
his tawny complexion lion wind and death
and waking dawn had still not blushed forth
and from the sheets I withdraw my pronominal self
a school-boy a vagrant among the early classics
a pupil of asterisk and circumflex I had
not yet understood how the gods portray themselves
in swords and clouds and hieroglyphs
tender as leaf and dew I sought to revise
each line that lay before me to be translated
each syllable accompanied by its macron or hiatus
each puzzling contour of noise from the beyond
was India in the context of each underlining ?
where was the cave that gives birth to shadows ?
what was the process of scanning but the effort
to remember what went before birth ?
come sunrise the envelopes fell away and
dim hills of reality were brought to bear
the invention of the telephone and the girlfriend
simultaneous events in the dark trajectory
the way to school and afternoons in the hive
the passage in and out of a single vowel
meant to be pronounced as if it were a ritual
to imagine priests giving sense to the holy syllable
alluding to the routine of hours as naught
how dull the senses compared to the One
which is neither life nor death but Afar !
legend rippled through the pages at my fingertips
evocations of the sacred moment called *Agape*
had I only known what that really meant symbol and pole
of the opposites no mind can resolve
Advaita ! to see in the casual step and gait
of the woman passing through glass a *goddess*
and like the hero bereft on the Libyan shore

to marvel that cities come and go !
could I but remember what Hari said
his inimitable chords his conch and whisk-broom
driving pairs of supreme white stallions
through the immense void of the Battle
school-boy ! naïve and innocent of reflection
anticipation of the enormous parenthesis
that contains an instantaneous future
the non-existent but for the steps and smoke
and the gunning motors of adolescence
lipstick of eternity and cigarettes !

04-27-20

THE SEPULCHER OF MEMORY

pale serene the placid line that crosses sleep's
meadow inadvertent clause of silence before
the radiance and suppose each of us were to be
again in other selves remembering some small
blade of grass evoking eternity but what of
the *else* the opposite side of darkness perimeter
of sound and dew sliding off into memory
and just who in the mirror is the self looking back
the cloak and hair and cosmetic rearrangement
the poem itself echoing rock fragment and pool
the small place where divinity steps to bathe
the singing in one ear only and the vast of space
shot through with punctuations of fiery dots
replacing each sentence uttered with a thought
that cannot be represented all as the other of
disbelief were we ever such as that roaming
pinnacle and dale in search of a mount to bear
us into the home of light to gather some twigs
kindling and a vocabulary to give fire its name
and emblazoned high the bright firmament of
sky etching courses where invisible chariots wing
burdened with the gravity of gods those puzzling
entities of force and graft shooting missiles
into the human mind inscriptions oracles and
the indecipherable secret of what can never be
so 'tis you and I and they and pronouns of repute
transgressions of person and mask speech acts

meant to bring statues to life and breath that
clings to air and hope and its resonance in
the charity of vowels ringing like clarions in
the dark and yes we ask the utter question
how and why and where did you ? and looking
askance the earth rotates off its axis and dreams
where we search for what it is we left behind

04-27-20

NIBBANA

standing on the Ganges' other bank eyes
turned inward to the nether floe and high
a resonance of sky and plunging light
all of time encapsulated in a single moment
when fire kindles a throw of vowels and
whatever went before is written on a consonant
repeated ad infinitum with faces of rapture
a robe of dismantled grace the corpse Invisible
made permanent in the noontime glare
let us praise the great circumflex and asterisk
the heavenly bodies that make aware the day
star bright and moon dust the powders oriental
the cinnamon and coral the peppermint and thyme
and most sandalwood of all the fragrances divine
an anklet bestowed by epic and bracelets forty
on each arm and ear-rings the size of satellites
that circle the planet of unknown Mind and
opened eyes again espy the wavering minaret
the mists and wafers and crimson monsoon winds
that bear mountains from the south and tongues
that no one understands and hour is now
for the Prayer and the signifier of the root
barefoot naked and living on orange goop
mendicants and rishis and animal avatars of Vishnu
annihilate living trust and swarm the broken temples
looking for a niche in the hundred-storey sculpture
depicting monkey graces and drunken elephants
charging unmanned godly chariots the thought !
the brain and design of water that descends
in a rush from Himalayan peaks to flood
the human plan and when waking is a thing

to do consider the various paths of sight
underneath matted groves of bright vermilion hues
or swarming over hummocks sacred to the bees
or winging in the dappled air of after-life
ethereal memories of who we were when we traveled
listing from bank to bank on the Ganges' fetid plain
floating face-up like lotuses red and blue
the eternal river-current lost in space and time
the ringing din in ears of stone
and hands tattooed with sound
the leaf that speaks in silence
the unbroken one of Two

04-27-20

MNEMOSYNE

I know you as Mnemosyne
who descend each dawn from the mountain
with the dew and like the dew disappear
chasing after the new-born light
as Mnemosyne herself vanishing memory
echo of rock and water that runs underneath
voice that trails as Mnemosyne in the winds
that leaves interpret with their tiny wails
noun and pronoun and larger words that linger
in the morning air a frost or a tribulation
of desires spent before the second hour
and I too am that undergone soul lost
in the wood beyond the hill listening for
the pale vowels of Mnemosyne the evanescent
and skies that tumble like washed sheets to dry
above the sleeping heads of statues
marmoreal essences fragments of the archaic
arcadian emblems shrouded in Mnemosyne's
distant syllables grass woven with fingers
attributes of a mythic hand that gestured high
in the empyrean to create the constellations
fierce and fiery asterisks and roving flares
the mind itself searching for its lexicon
Mnemosyne who can you ever be other than
the sound re-created of the earliest thought
enigmatic booms sent like powders on the turf

as if to open tombs of light and incandescence
where the dead have gone before their time
Mnemosyne as the dew that draws its breath
from its own disappearance and leaves no shape
no husk no hue nor dappled tone a gone
thing like the world at large the immense
invisibility that involves each passing form
do you take these hands Mnemosyne
do you embrace the figment of speech
addressing you ? I call upon you
to remember this the only *poem* !

04-28-20

THREE STANZAS ON AN EPIPHANY

far trekking star-sighter the wain that
lumbers by Orion's chase a globe at a time
a fist held bright beyond the eye's lonesome
view held like summer in a small crystal ball
either the twain or his utter lain to rest in
the gypsy coffin bark lettered and scripted
in as many tongues mind can kindle firing
at memory for a loss the penny-whistle candle
the orient at once larger than ink aspiring
to rise its own sun and the belt around its
brow wrapped tight the fierce and aching
to grieve along and not stop chance to spread
as does shedding the lamp its glister frayed
how fuse the thongs ! the weary wasted thought
inch by worm the fledgling post and blasted
bleaker than the worst moment's course
cannot the bleeding cease the carcass wound
a whole within its diameter the round a moon
as it plies the celestial surf its backside burns
to know what memorial drives the months
off the bidden haste and Lo ! riven and creased
the rock we held the hand that threaded grass
the finding and its twilight in despair 'tis home
ward bound the ancient brother his river side
his mirage mirror marked the sidelong glance
is me too a flux lingering ripple tide a song so
loud no sparrow can withstand and larks hove

into the provençal sky of *trobar clus* the clouds
dizzy the shifting whites and dreamers blanks
blanched a face in the crowd a far remove from
dwelling the place asleep is most the heavy stone
ear and pestle the mortal clue to die is whilom
the fuming disregard down to the ships to sail

if you say it in Italian it's nine times bigger and
three stone-weight more if it sorrows haunting
but girls get the grist of it moaning forms a link
to beyond hills are laments that fade westerly
the gloaming of shift and tangle sparks debate
in trance wearing a top hat and lustrous boots
tippled hinting at the maroon and ocher paints
highlighting the school walls fifty or more years
back in the Neolithic ballroom of slow-dance
shadow sifted remembrances crooner in blazer
dust jacket corporate spine title book report
due this Friday O three of the meridian and
Joe sucking his thumb over Gide or Camus a
window on the woods when darkening comes
and no one to hold and crying secretly footnoted
in a sequence of dots to the far right margin
holding a finger up and watch it bleed the poster
of lives long past the gone ceremony of tuck and
gait chasing through the man-tall corn to the south
where abandoned the many and unknown dead
fry a melancholy if ever and to understand the
very first of Dante or the hunting in Avernus
or whatever etchings come out of a Latin verb
you have to listen ear to the side of the highway
to diesels creating in their roar a mysterious
night of far away and never was

just as short is broken for sadness all the round
a month that passes for a day glassed and voiced
with only two vowels ere nightfall and the whim
of the sidereal show as we lay backside looking
out of our skins triplicate panorama in carbon
papered and suited for a section of air painted
over because of the circularity of heat imposing
darkened moments in July and sounds lapping
of the pool where the electric fishes of the fathers
ply finny and resounding like kids leaping from

the high diving board wasn't that a solar splash
knees held tight eyes shut to fate roller frictions
as it goes so does the underside and reefing slow
smoke that bluish curls from under lip the nostrils
flaring wide a god must have been there somewhere
in the greenery intimate with alcoholic subterfuge
luring tenderly the souls slipping into glass flashing
and held high the questioning hand to revolve its
planetary digits the famous inkling of death
hidden in the leaf and the barking three-headed
dog named Duke and slight and wisp of a thing
the nymph whose broad brown eyes all seeing
as matters pass from view into the great bubble
atmospheric and mysterious as clouds uncontained
flight ! parsing verbs person mood and number
shouting ! a single blade of grass and call that
infinity ! all hangs by a single hinge the door
going back and forth the echo sound of rubber
tires smoothing over gravel three in the morning
what an enigma the truce of being alive for
just that moment to hear that crunching sound
relieved at last that they have come home

04-29-20

IN LOVE WITH LOVE

star-wimple and fade the downy crest you were
ever the ribbing in my side always the almagest
to read by night skilled paper foils a word at a
but wasn't that your error making way through
wood and maze a fiction doubled in your image
and the paste and mortar the fling of clouds in
disappearing ink the very firmament smoking
at the top of the stairs beside you my little One
whereas in small print the ledger divides by two
we seek to cruise we delve to drive the sun-cart
just you and egoless me first and last-most at
your backside riddled by the puzzle of your being
stung by the innards of conscience and pelted
dust storming across the western hills longing
forever to otherwise be the strength and till of
your desire I remain as faithful your always

signed the undertow of tide rushing moons
your extinct passion bud the flowering bloom
of atavistic splendors white-side thrill ruddy
as the dawn's fingerlings dew-touched by grass
by your hose I am drawn by the silver patter
of night-speech deriving from nowhere cluster
of consonants on the tongue's numb sweeping
oracle and light ! the yes of afterthoughts dense
darning of celestial bodies in song amazingly
the bright of each diphthong in cursive script
and written loud the intensity it was at your
slide by the lamp of fireflies wick and candle
peaceable kingdom in sheets unfolding hues
come morn and sorrowing in the glittering
fade of the last and removed fixed planets
from their orbits and Diana on the chase argent
of ankle and of the nomadic waist who recalls
with even ears the echo of the roaring solar wind
as it was and ever will be 'til leaf us resound
the twain in the forest primeval the archaic
rock the standby drill by the holy well and shades
dancing the round of love's epistles lost aghast
the fuming and tardy air circling counter clock
wise the fission in each thumb the nail and fuse
passed the month of epithalamium and reddened
the crease between our brows and eying the gilt
tasseled hair in your part of the world Oh Bright
thou as pronouns go and still I pursue your feet
ivy-twined and colored like floating lotuses across
the ire-green surface of the Pond to drown
face-down the thing of a heart transpierced for
ever by Cupid's wingless dart a flame a fire a
Breath for an instant only and to vanish within
you and be held on the altar of your sacrifice
beating vein pulse and anatomy of the *Invisible*

04-29-20

DIDO & AENEAS

with pictured breast held forth the tow of words
did aim his shaft and burrowed it deep within
underwent then the tide of sounds echoing
in ears soon filled with water a dream he spoke
when all the marble listened was great the woe
the sandwiched grief between illicit hours a height
to reach of sense if not the mountain of peril
is life on earth worth this gain hands fluttered
in rhetoric of shapes and addressed the queen
whose idiom bespoke eyes of torment and sorrow
did recall other treacheries the somnolent gravity
of worldly affairs passing like a purple thunderhead
over the assembly and would Harmony but intervene
and the caustic beauty of the consort of Zeus wavering
a sylph of a thing in disguise interring her counsel
in the adversity of fate et cetera did then hexameter
roll after hexameter and the bruiting shifts of tone
and elision and parenthetical remark and asterisk
about to explode in the clarity of day the azure
vault and its tombs of distance and ire and the *Poet*
reckoning his courtly attire and the wish to burn
whatever he had inscribed to memory as if his
presence mattered and the silken pleats and wines
poured by some invisible handmaid and tables
of dainties and slaves frowning behind curtains
can ebony and emerald come together and yet
his peroration the account of a troubling deceit
fixed forever in the annals and what's to come
the next day when school starts and the skirts
taken by the winds whose great shadows blow
over the incandescent seas of prophesy of course
and he returns her gaze and meadows of verdant
hope as they say to wait for the embrace and eventide
or seek a cave to hide out the storm according to
the movie script and his brazen glance and her ardent
tumult of echoes in italics and speaking if she could
had not Venus in her irreverent intrusion
quelled all expectation but that of the pyre
do then all things come to smoke and tears

04-30-20

LACHRYMAE RERUM

this aching truth of life blind as steel
to endure one day more day after day
with no power to turn back and even less
to foretell the fated hour why then not
fall into a blowzy dream and retire
from chores that wind us back and forth
nuisance and routine the sounding bell
marking each minute that we breathe
with dread sense of naught the wheel
that spins fruitlessly the iron that sleeves
burn and shirtless the ghost arrays who
appears to us pleading to re-run the trial
that robbed him of mask and person and
sent to Avernus straight a wight such as
he we might all be and traverse the *hour*
none the less wishing to cloud the mind
and sleep that tideless flow underneath
whence none return whom we grieve
what hap what unasked for accident
set us in this dismal house to travail ?
did winsome loss of past a face reveal
the whites of destiny underpinning whole
the remainder of the rites of breath and
to what avail the inchworm glowing loud
the farther side of the shadow open wide
glimpses of a contour resembling heaven's
tale the asterisk and progeny of vowels
endless sound of talking in a former ear
how silent the grisly oak blasted by a bolt
from Jove sent to spear some foolish heart
resounding knell the baying hounds of hell
choice mention of chance to flee this vale
to round the bend the summer down under
can no one read this running flow of ink
mottled decibel and raging letter zed ?
has done with thinking now the raveled bee
whose sting implies some greater mind at work
a lesson never learnt an afternoon ill spent
drugged and by the window declaiming wild
the final consonant and hands tripped up
and shapes of evanescent airs the glove that

dies the thumb gone wrong and last the one
laments the flowered hills now sheltered
in the darkness of a single yearning leaf

05-01-20

THE CREATIVE WRITING CLASS

penned a note late night to Eliot or Pound
was awake counting quoits the universe along
and clued Joyce whispering in the mold
his western dream of rising soon and lived
enough to tell as I learned to write an
alphabet and choicest of the sounds an echo
did renown a staff and pike a note the wireless
round and fifty times or more lunations
that I spent quilling a lover's note in ire to
learn and form the spelling asterisks afar
who could speak as I had spoke that afternoon
last spring in the high school choir a hand
I used to riddle codes of ancient Mycenean
confounded Mayan glyph with Etruscan tomb
the mirror backwards dangling by a thread
and red became in plenty and the fuse and
fear implied each mind as it turned to
vacate its lodge and whiten the cloven spire
alas dear dead the deafer you did grow gave
no taint to my nascent spark nor puzzle
to my intent as scripts went raveling about
sweet Luna's pyre and buttressed between
archaic vowel and tone the heights of stone
the running that burns underneath and sleep
a maze that fools imply will offer truths afloat
nay did the class return their gaze and wonder
what I meant when I imitated Priam in his web
and sent Hector spinning like a top dustier
than the spider in his grave and Look ! I aspired
pointing to the calendar in its Italianate rotund
no day is greater than this Night I spent penning
verses to Villon and Petrarch in a Frankish tongue
darkest woods and deeper still the gravid idiom
of grief and sorrows a million dread and girls
in their summer hose who averted eyes of flame

me they saw no more but a shadow of fustian
lore the caustic and drill of language the bore
that finds in rock the spirit to endure time's knot
talking as statues do when noon has lost its heat
and to cold marble they return loose verses
chiseled from the Ionian shore and lasting
through middle hours of the dark the fingers
that weep removing grass from Achilles' shield
the cosmos whole no more and fiery whispers
none understand but the ear that belongs to none
sand breakers surf and waves of blackening
and horses running mad along the beach and
brains in their labyrinth recalling virgin myths
about the Faerie Queen and oblivion on the page
no library could withstand what I had to say
and what I had to say was naught a syllable
caught between vast samples of light unborn
this much I to Pound or Eliot did pen and to
Joyce I gave reply as to why the Wake and
as to forever misunderstand death's rattle
multiple like the sound of leaf and stone

05-01-20

THE TOMB OF LIGHT

death and memory have the same origin
death and memory have the same origin
so we hear the statues say surveying the park
and playing field where the kids lie strewn
all over the place lifeless and beautiful in
their finery jewels and garlands of lotus and iris
glitter of blood sparkling in the heavy noontime sun
and the whirring in the air of invisible things
deities or demons in a contest for their souls
night comes and goes in a wink with its panoply
of *deathless* stars and light itself struggles
to maintain a face in the odds of annihilation
come on over and let's play war !
junior high school intermittence and the togs
and handlebars and bike wheels and strumming
a broken guitar in the basement the entire
world of innocence and books left out to dry

and the moon rotating from its red self
to its pale and ghastly other self at the crossroads
and below the bridge where the river runs out
and the white wraiths with the bodies of naked women
who have returned to stake their claim on breath
it is morning over and over and the sorrow
ignited in bar-room jukeboxes and spilling over
on the pavement where hooded thugs wait to lynch
the commander-in-chief and his wives and
wagers on the horse race tomorrow and fans
and flags and fluttering gloves that make air dense
when will we understand why it happened ?
kings nourished on pride and silks mourn sons
whose wick was snuffed too soon and rishis ply
repeatedly the loom of truths about desire
and attachment and the brooding afterworld
and even today yes today when the unseen germ
runs rampant through mortal flesh and piled up
in refrigerated cars the unnamed and unclaimed
when will we understand that even *light*
has an end and can be buried anonymously
in an Etruscan potters' field ?

05-02-20

IN THE MERRY MONTH OF MAY

by what uneven syntax does the worm hold sway ?
macromolecular demons unraveling the script of time
each day release distortions of mind and thought
and flowers born just at dawn now bend their necks
in sweet decay the ever was of the world the height
once scored to be at hand the distance gained is
now fourfold lost and traffic both ways denies
the sun its total grace of shine and what is it you
demand standing in your store-bought line a brace
of hounds some meal to feed the dying cattle or
simply a new ring for your fading mate ? songs
there are for times like this and ballads silent
as the morning dew and remembrances of souls
stolen from the bright of day and whatever else
mortal plight stains with unaccustomed hue and pain
will not subside but grief increase and sorrow sow

among the rushing grasses yearning for precious light
do seas hold sway thundering against the fief of rock ?
does purple mountain haughty and lone desire to fly ?
what of this earth this paltry blue-gassed history of rags
fictions of weave and tear the myths of come-again
and losses by the millions over epochs doomed with glory
which of the several continents will be first to submerge ?
do we hear at last fragile voices buried in the leaf ?
what do their small vowels declaim against such winds
that uproot temple dome and rows of sacred trees ?
will we breakfast ever again in some cliff-side inn that
clings to earth's edge overhanging a paradise of waves ?
remember that sunset in Big Sur when all the cosmos
seemed wrapped in a flare most gorgeous of evanescent
red and nothing of substance escaped that taint ?
the ocean is a breath away and the islands of remote
where bells and husks and titled bones gather in the dusk
a gloaming of unpaid tithes the worry and burden
that tasks mortals plunging them into a black surf
where the original seed feeds on its own demise
nor eye nor ear nor memory itself retain anything
but echoes of death's tattooed daughter *oblivion*

05-03-20

THE DAY YOU WOKE FROM A DREAM OF SHADOWS MOVING MYSTERIOUSLY THROUGH THE TOMB OF SOUND YOU LEARNED TO MEMORIZE THE ANCIENT VOWELS AND THENCE TO HAP UPON DEATH'S SMALL DOOR

at last the alluvial running under and the leaf at first
the only outline in the dark and the soul infirm of
shape lacking fuse the slender lamp its face betrays
air and winds whirling in memory's ear a fading
finally of grass and fingers beneath working loam
and the talk of tiny worlds and ears that only silence
hear and the biggest cloud of all that passes through
the eye leaving summer's lonely mark of pallid red
and the job of bringing it all together and lying
there half dead and half awake windows full of stars
asterisks throbbing from afar the loneliness then
the sheer wonder if another such as you is there

to trek the vast direction of this disordered depth
be there a poem a sound a lyric of unrecorded notes
whatever aroused you from the brink and tossed
the unholy hint the reckless quoit of noise and youth
it was that thin and distant roaring of celestial wheels
the traffic of disfigured gods or angels yearning
to be loud and transient and oracular and mistaken
all at once the words that took form in languages
barely kenned and with them sped down highways
to cities unmapped and violent with mysteries beyond
the pale a cinema of illicit cutup and temple ruins
where women bathed in numinous saliva wander
with their million years of hair the inky mosses in
their eyes and unsighted lovers in rocky glens and lost
like enigmas you can only touch in the immensity of sleep
for far from this single point this growth of mind
tender as the newest breeze on budding bloom alight
fast as you could rise that spring dawn to espy chasing
on the lawn a fleeting doe the goddess Diana herself
of nimble ankle and purity of form a mirage divine
a poem's introduction a guide to the labyrinthine day
to come the heights and blowzy splendor of sun-bright
issuing acclamations of the unseen event and hosts
of disembodied voices the heavenly denizens of verse
your hand a pen seized and unconscious words poured
forth the unlimited thought it seemed that crazed
your dazzled brain a freshet and springs of parnassan
water and hills that composed the western *mysteries*
with song and leaves and tree-tops clinging to the dark
a vision to be inscribed if only memory kept her vow
and with the flight of oneiric birds and their latin song
your moving fingers delved in the maze of sounds
comes down then the holy vowel the trebled accent
the imagined bone-text the chiseled glyph and sign
adumbrations of sacred scripts untold the many
to be discovered your day of reckoning the shining most
the alpha and its sequences of rhyme and tumbling from
the cloudy brow of the perfect divinity pure inspiration
your baedekker to the fragments of antiquity and light
how much you underscored the ensuing disorder and
of chaos made a number that multiplied equals nine
the Muses in their sorority of distance and echo a shimmer
instantaneous confusing past and present the Orphic *now*

when unconscious rock feels the sorrow of longing
grief of separation and turbulence of unexpected loss
so you learned and tried to memorize what is best left
forgotten in the mummery of human life you turned
and looked upon the lawn and by your side a brother
too was felt weeping shoulder and knee against a door
to remain unopened until the end of time

05-04-20

PROGNOSIS : ZERO

we will next time be gone forever though the scribes
who live on borrowed air think otherwise
and the tenses of the archaic verb unfold a ladder
with broken roses at the top and that reaches
only half way to *there* a poignant leaf of echoes
to dally in the presence of a *god* who's gone begging
up and down he goes with half-thought verbiage
on his illicit tongue to nag the senators for a mouth
of rice a fly-whisk a dram of vinegar and the heavens
multiple at first the radiance of a single sun-bright ray
all days are come to *this* uncountable and hallucinatory
who is behind the other door drying the muse's braid ?
come search the realm of fireflies and set up the screen
long nights without consent face down in solitude
each has no other and the half is scorned for its lack
waking is no promise but a semi-conscious dare to see
and what's out there beyond the glassy hills of illusion
a lark a tree ready to fall blasted by a withering bolt
to understand surfaces are uni-dimensional as the seers
are wont to say and fuse and fission alternate
each thumb missing a hand and tossed into the fire
a dozen or so letters from a smuggled alphabet
smoking desire the ultimate key-stroke a vowel
inches from its own eternity and the longing
not to know but to *forget* and the scorched plains
the lost grasses the wild-flowers blown away
my heart ! they all cry my devastated *heart* !
come plunging into seething inks harsh consonants
school-book grammars and heating pipes and
lintels approached by shadowy figures that must
in another world tarry and what of the discourse

among the *thinkers* gathered by the empty pools
and vats and the ivy decaying around their temples
and what was shining the once and plenitude
is now grief the worn knees and shabby sloping backs
mantels and cloaks moth-eaten the drivel of talk
back and forth fly words consumed by ambiguity
the *this* which has long past the *that* which is nowhere
and winding cursive roads and rock fragments
and the torment of twilight hues staining mountain
and sea alike and the losses innumerable and
what do the *authors* say about their destroyed works ?
lost in the *selva oscura* and night the incommensurable
the accident of time ! birth and death of memory
space yawning beyond its limits unbroken silence

05-05-20

THE FALL OF TROY

> "Tum vero omne mihi visum considere in ignis
> Ilium et ex imo verti Neptunia Troia"
> *Aeneid, II, 624–625*

watching it all fall rotted timbers roofs burning
come plunging into the silt and loam and ghosts
just recently sent from the here-and-now still
roaming hungry bloodshot eyes begging cup
held out in the fumes and mists and barefoot
the daughters fearing for their hair running
helter skelter lest the crashing walls bar the way
hoodwinked by the gods just inches from paradise
and the trident that overturns and the glaucous
waves higher than a hero's brow rushing into
the cinders where smolder the souls of kings
the exit is the entrance to Hades and loud accents
and pitched vowels and the drawl and spore
of broken consonants every one trying to express
and utter at the same time their experience of the end
and to take the hand of one who is no longer there
and to lay the head turned to stone on hot ash
raining from the hidden cicatrix of heaven
how fierce the ululation from floors far underneath
white-phantom wraiths in blanched tatters
unbearable the weeping and the children lost

between the pedestals of angry statues and rock
and flinty slabs of unnamed stone quarried from
memories of those gone down in long black ships
to listen for the spiral of bees in their wild innuendo
like a song from the realms of distance Echo her
sobbing litanies ricocheting between the plastered
incongruencies of script and oracle that amass
in the densely smoking air and altars fresh
with sacrifices eyes and skulls intent on light which
no longer exists but dusky plasma and the coal-dark
absences of those forgotten by their own names
AIYEE the *Erinyes* with their formulas for revenge
tearing nouns of substance into finite shells of air
the loudest a lament from the poet whose faltering
syllables and trailing hexameters ravel in the gloaming
so much for the splendors of the dithyramb and trochee
the fabled seas of gilt-edged pages that roll on
to western shores and mountains with purple masses
of myth and music all fading on the promontory
of extinct gasses the cosmos revolving inanely
around itself as the *Lamp-of-Asia* goes extinct
no more the maddened remembrances of glory only
soft nightfall when shaking leaves lose their voice

05-05-20

AFTER DAYS OF INANITION AND TRANCE THE MUSE PLANTS A SEED IN VIRGIL'S MIND

as from a fleeting dream I sought the mountains
came and went the passing souls whose embrace
was a vanity and unconscious the words of grief
and sorrow like winds from the eastern banks
half-shattered syllables vowels in retreat the smaller
connections of echo and silence whatever to mind
brought some sense of memory and then waking
spent on a bark adrift in the colloquy of waters
found the self peeled from the other self and waiting
for dawn's first attributes the resonance of wave
and hoof and petals damp with dew slowly dropping
into immersions of shadow and distance the hand
took the text and in the new bluish air of the unknown
provoked the day with an invisible script penning

from the beyond what thoughts could gather their
immense immobility and to the heavens up I looked
and still the cloud frame and unseen thunder and rays
magnificent with the promises of Apollo what was
that ? another day in a world of rocking sensibilities
of reaching for a direction no stylus had ever discovered
the phrases the intimations of a verse the locutions
connecting deity to myth and insane references to
half-recalled incidents the field strewn with untenanted
armor and circling in the dazzle above birds of prey
ominous diction of the fates weird voices wings flapping
consonants that embroidered the eyelids of the dead
monuments of dust pulverized grain statues weary
of holding their heads up the slightest motion to over-
come ! how did I come to be floating alone on this
reverie of waves and sun-glint the glassy surfaces
of the Middle Sea rocking slowly an imagery of cities
drowned in a trice in some orient of flying tapestries
and turrets and domes and alphabets intricate as
the *thing* the eye sees sleeping on the wharf of dreams
awake ! I am and penning this cribbed intimation of
an epos of wordless spaces of antiquities of childhood
of the deaths and finalizations of leaf and shrub
the edges and the centers confused between commas
and the futile asterisks of burning and salvation
exhumed the mind the flaring lamps of the Muse
the flowering altars !

05-06-20

MUSING ON ONE'S BRIEF MORTALITY

for among others jack and neeli

an old man works his crazy quilt verses from
yore and adolescence his fingers weave still young
thoughts aberrant and twice-told myths the tales
that fertilize the mind his gnarled hands abuse
the morning breeze and like a prayer hail the rising
beams and curtails nothing of swift running lines
across the virgin page the glories of an epic still
untold the hold on imagination of grove and glade
the tolling distance of a bell and still sorrowing
re-works sadder yet the deepest moments of his life

revealed and disclosed between curtains darker still
the unreaped grasses of the waving fields where
once walked he and his nymph of ether bright
and rills and throngs of echoing syllables in a tongue
dredged from forest leaf and running brook a
music his oriental brain perceives and wonders
sounding it around bends of ancient cliff and woof
reveries of cosmic seconds that last an eternity
and brother and son and dumbfounded entities
that grapple with harsh destinies on the turning wheel
flames and days that pass in hotels of vacant rooms
and chambers where each the other hopes to find
dwelling in the brassy containment of the unheard note
a ringing clash of vowels in archaic dialects and stone
the whispering immobility and fragments of water
and inches from heaven's portal the abscess of thought
that returns to him repeatedly the self-same story
the spear and shield and mantras of divinity withheld
can so many years be encompassed in the thumb
that shakes minutely in its diapason of immortality
does it become age and its decades of flickering light
to continue exploring alphabets and glyphs of dew
ethereal continents that verge like letters of drying ink
to evanesce and wither unremembered forever more ?
how many doors left to open how many windows
without blinds or shades how many anything to
recount in the dim and dazzle of consciousness
that lasts no more than the flash of a passing bolt ?
05-06-20

THE AUTOMATIC STONE

as much as the fact frilled with writing
is a fist full of ink lettered beside the all
knowing kink in the rubric of time is it no
matter the while I speak so aphasic the drone
drilled of statues in a tongue little hewn
from marble it's still only just that a quill
styles the whole with dots speckled like
asterisks on the quilt's holy night-scape the
lasting ever tombstone of flint with aleph
as props to talking asleep to the dangerous
graphs of fire all hair razing and fifth from

the right the unlettered boy his blaze a fan
of ivory toys and hands out reached to grasp
the purploy of antiquity's apostrophe to keep
within the photo's small frame and leaf and
twine the twins I mean whom dust cannot
deploy nor distinguish by rote the envelope
taught at sunrise and buried by sundown
each is the number of every and one escapes
being two by a darker third the stuttering
finger dials its grass for a telephonic moan
alas the murmur of his girl the friend at first
a pram of delights four-wheeled as all night-
sleeps dreaming are in rotation of sounds until
stone's whisper is the echo fulfilled in clouds
scudding summer-long beneath the ear and
what could be greener more filled with bees'
must the oval hive of sky the teeming with seas
that pour through the text's boneyard of signs
what's written was there by the door-yard's gate
smaller and dewy the way the goddess retrieved
her first steps and put them in air for all to revise
her verses and undressed the top of her hair a
comb and a style all empress as turning afternoons
in heat and circular red the fan of her face inching
toward denial as so it was ampersand and all
that fateful yes when the author penned his plot
coils and sumps of the western mire a waste land
a cycle of pivots on the backside of the moon a
lunatic avarice with inscriptions in old Toltec
the spoke and the modicum of a burning wheel
crossing its own atlantic the heraclitean Mile
if you listen and crave and jot down each lisp
and tone each of four accents a history in meter
at lost the longing a leaf by the door a rock
underneath and her blanched knees Persephone
comes back up to earth grass-stained and parched
for a drink of rebirth steeps and takes a breath
token of madness the smile of her writ big
as the lunar sound for O and then resides
mid the fireflies whose grace is the whole of air
and flying fast the final silence a pitch of fours
vedic and resonant as the stolen quiet of the waves
a gleaming weave of sonant glyphs the tumulus

in Etruscan for archaic patience and lore
a dream at the wheel a crash and no more

05-06-20

END-GAME

could not see at the first the winding down
the news in echoes of still another famous death
tribulations in tiny waters glimmering in dreams
that no eye beholds for long and back to shoals
of sleep returns in undulations of black tides
the former life where has it gone the childhood
rebuked by parasol and mummery of chance ?
what game is ever played that is truly fair ?
your side must win and mine must lose however
divided we have the world between us
yet you've long gone aloft on wings of distance
and the dust you left behind the small burning
whorls of evanescent memory what are they
but cavities in the air I breathe redundancies
of space and time ? locked in an embrace
with ghosts and specters ruminations of a voice
cavernous and incoherent that rocks the mind
words and less than words the halves of a lost
syllable that lingers in the springtime breeze
yearning with remembrances and false starts
the engine that will never run again the pedal
and meter and extensions of archaic verse
the uselessness of the featured star last night
the blinking dot dot dot of misinterpreted code
the vast array of stellar messages we once read
of a brilliant summer night guessing which was
the passage and which the dead-end of *time*
today what's worse I simply do not know
and run my fingers through the grass hoping
to somehow find your fingerprints and allay
for a moment the dreaded sense of no-more
the way we fretted in the church yard about
immortality and picking up our dusky selves
sought to return to the map we'd drawn
not a city but a necropolis of smoke and ash
empty houses addresses that have been erased

wherever we had been and walked a mere
mirage the aching vowel of a lost eternity

05-07-20

ECHOES ONLY ECHOES

the ear remembers echoing through stone
the density of dreams and oblivion of sleep
the heights once and across the roiling waves
spent days in unrecalled travail the youthful
sparring with wind and storm the greenery
that bound the temples in life's springtime
while a voice from afar dictated verse and tune
the prosody of mountain-born meter and
scansion syllable by syllable of pure poesy
remembers in the still and winding chamber
that leads into the middle-brain a moment
loud with life and heat the puissant battery
of love's sweet game the back and forth of
light that shone down from the source and
made noise among the shadows bantering
and bickering in the fraught hours of breath
who would gain and who lose the thread that
guides and how many the losses come mid-term
when already to look back and account are
to no avail and it is only grief that makes
sense unwinding the bitter accents of a failed
effort a gesture with hands invisible to reach
the ringing bell whose lost afternoon still
resounds and the lengthening shades and
faltering leaf the whispering caught unawares
when the streets dead-end and trees surround
the ruin of a play-yard the empty swings
a slope and soft turf and the reading of
the *text* when gathered around the myth
the many now half-nameless who listened
to words spun out of hives and oracles
warnings of the end and to sleep again
in rock and inter the ear's memory of bliss

05-08-20

THE TIME OF OUR LIVES !

from what corrupt hall of envy and fame
does this day's sorrow issue what tarnished
names what lack of dignity warping dreams
all around the shattered maypole vestiges
of rope and tassel echoes of former joys
footsteps that lead only half-way back to
brighter hours lacking edges the boundless
cannot be reused the words once winged that
flew off the line from oracles and fictions
up drove the consonants from their bed
darker hush at first the lesser droning
sounds that usher in day's frayed decline
often hills and again deeper the groves and
glens shaded by some musk or oriental clime
desert and waste the hearts of men the billowing
swarms of locust the maddened wasps that
make of air a perilous chaos the very lamp
that shone now noontime's blackest orb
swirling in a miasma of perjury and theft
this they say is the world plight the result
of unchecked histories of mayhem and greed
this the inheritance and gift of Prometheus
whom gods have forsaken and left to wither
on the rock and wild sessions of anemone
and burr and clouds pumped up with ire
derail whole seasons of their plenitudes
markets of rot and soiled garments glare
the afternoon's forbidden moments painted
in slabs of pitch and leaking oils the foulest
disregard for beauty's outer shine the dazzle
and what's to gain by improprieties and curse
language bedimmed by ignorance and ruin
all around the stuttering and stammering
of statues in reverse and engines employed
by racketeers of the nation state ring loud
drilling the ear with sophistries of vengeance
and promises of flying to planet Mars
++++++++++++++++++++++++++++++++
no more say but stay the mind's distress
the curlicues and epithets of lore that vague
into the winds scatter like uttered charms

vast memory in her dappled raiment of legend
and dancing lights and consternation overpowers
the fleet foot of the graces three and monuments
of ethereal distances myths of unspoiled innocence
that dwell in a mansion of imperishable echo
syllables of unheard notes and a music green
as the leaf born in the morning dew and sung
in bird chants across rearing peaks of azure
the once and only of the library the tale
of countless Saturdays of immutability
where is the world gone in such display
and why do the avenues turn dark running
against the grain of infirmity ? release the hand !
let fly the wing that takes its place into heights
that are the threshold of a new and infinite thought
the dying soul's attainment of far beyond
among the asterisks and kindling of the stars
where depths are *light* and light itself the *dark*
surrounding the great nothingness of space
AMEN!

05-09-20

AENEAS

as a *sign* I saw four white horses grazing
peacefully by the temple of Minerva
voices echoing from the shore exultant waves
a distance hazy volcanic peak lifting its white plume
high into the stratosphere another *sign*
a petition to the gods and putting on her make-up
cerulean and roseate Venus who was about
to make a mysterious presence by my side
flanks of sacrificial oxen promised no sooner
should we land here and shaking her tresses
silver-foil surf-drenched enticing glances
up and down the hemisphere felt
the earth gliding slowly away under my feet
was dreaming that the fires and ruin were behind
and all I had to do was stretch my hands out
still the rumbling of the sea-god the earth-shaker
emoluments to his resting places and motels
would wake up after a definitive trance

in the nether world questing in footsteps after
the *fathers* who I was and what childhood
had been allotted to me and whence this aching
dolorous heart I bore with desire for unknown
was it a poem an exercise in versification
the dark wrapped first around my knees
other days to come in a brief sunlit yard
kneeling with others and hearing loud
the weeping and transgressions of men
to build walls *here* turrets forty floors high
and to learn a new language one of flint
and basalt and rock fragments with writing
and prayers like smoke ascending from the vowels
as ancient as I had become a figment of literature
was overcome with the baleful sense
that no scripture could dispel this unconscious
and the flowers white and sparse and blue
lovely and tender in the early breeze was I
among them neck bent head heavy and shaking
lambent rays of light before me as I step
tottering in the meadow fragrant with honey
the bees circling in their swift consonants
and everything pell-mell dizzy spinning
out of sight this land I had taken as mine
slope edging purple the western occlusions
soft dappled twilight could I approach once more
the *signs* fallen from memory the burning
cities the arches and columns of sand and salt
the voyages across the glassy-surfaced sea
a single voice torn from the leaf
I still hold in my hand a sobbing in the ear
and night coruscating vanishing

05-10-20

THE LAUGHING BOY

you ask what death is and I tell you
death is this laughing boy whom
I cannot return to you is this leaf tender
green and trembling destined to wither
and fall is this face in the mirror yours
which when finished shaving will disappear
as well as the skirts worn by the nymphs
and the garlands earrings necklaces jewels
that adorn your girlfriends past and present
is this laughing boy I repeat I cannot give
him back cannot restore his breath is this
tree by the side of the house of memory
shaking in a late winter wind is this hand
from out of nowhere come to take your
books away your sheets of paper your inks
your very mind a thought at a time will
take you by the knees in a surfeit of darkness
is this sweet laughing boy you cling to
in fond and terrible remembrances that
I will not render is this folded air this sky
which is only a portion of what you see daily
is this poem you are writing in the balance
of the hours left to you is this moment
irretrievable and whatever else you hold
precious and dear like the laughing boy
in all his plastic insouciance his toys and
parades and streets of innocent red brick
the level of heights above his vanishing
the protocol of doctors and pharmacists
is this wholesale destruction of reality
bridges that go nowhere trampolines and
long asphalt roadways is death for certain
with its amphetamine crazed truck drivers
and insurgent rebels plotting to overtake and
what else is new on the day's agenda is death
waiting around the corner lurking in the eaves
is stepping lightly on the forbidden sidewalk
is taking this laughing boy this photo and
silhouette this stucco wall against which
rasps the plum tree branch in Chinese
poetry and the pink cherry blossoms is death

constantly paving clouds and shuttering
the places where light once shone through is
sleep and always abiding in the depths where
Orpheus has gone and the music is death
resounding beautiful echoes of solo violin
or flute on the hill is the phantom brother
lying there still in his orphanage of lamps
whom I cannot give back to you is the maps
you sketched on x-ray paper is the whistle
in the afternoon and the dog running to meet
you coming home from school is the alley
behind the many unknown houses is and
always is and cannot be denied the laughing
boy your boy whom no amount of mourning
will revive not today not ever is this
haunting you cannot remove from your
unbidden shoulders the cathedral of bones
that moves restlessly inside you is so much
and everything death laughing like a boy

05-11-20

THE GRASS-CUTTER

remember to look out for the sun his jet
black horses making a route in the sky and
to wait for the heat to complete its cycle
before the meridian and each stone in place
step lightly over the dewy fields and sing in
low voice hymns you learned to the goddesses
the many multiformed blessed divinities
of sweat and blindness the day ahead is
great with promise the grasses by the mile
to be mown and lain aside and bare of foot
and in droves the ones who come behind and
alert to the swarms of mosquitoes or bees the holy
sound that echoes in the cavity of air the lustrous
and glistening apparition of the One who
will illustrate the way and give aid if you fall
and call out the secret syllables and moist
the passage to the west where the dark houses
stand and the ghosts and remnants of rock
carved fragments of the Founders of heaven

itching in the palms eye throbbing ominously
storm clouds gathering at the junction of
light and time but don't look *there* avert
your gaze clumps of damp weeds in fistfuls
your mind kept on the task the direction
the chariots will take driving across the high
road the loss of kings of heroes the verses
straining to recollect call out what you can
of the services to the dead to the hosts who
have gone underground and forgot not
especially to call out to *Persephone* for her
appearance this June and decked with flowers
many-hued she will promise a new season
and the *return* before the great year moves
on the Wheel and beware the ant-hills like
traps in the soil and in sheaves lay the grasses
against the dry-well and be grateful for the
willow offering shade memory of mornings
in the *other place* when you were young and
about you nymphs assembled drying hair
in the fast breezes of the afternoon wasn't
that the time and your brother playing flute
and the invisible friends of love and time-flights
endless riot of the moment only to disperse
in the shrewd rains and aging that happened
so fast your locks grew gray your vision
bedimmed and still you call out for the others
to follow though none there are who really
remember you other than the one who weeps
so plaintively at twilight listening for phantom
herds nostalgia the nightfall of eternity

05-12-20

THE HEAD OF AVALOKITEŚVARA

we have seen from the writing and discourse
cursive elements borrowings from rock fragments
lunar disease ticks and mites inflected nouns
syllables partial and disregard the solar fractions
figments of mercy no word can fully express
ornamentation leading to individual style
the lap generous and full skirt unfolding her
gaze as dust and dew combined on proportion
of light in a time of aggravation be it now
or whenever by chance paper and stylus
palm-leaf and sudden transition to vocalic
and sensuous utterances depicted first in
cave paintings full-bodied women tanned and
embracing ethereal creatures vowels in name only
a rush of waters from the high peaks north
and as we have seen dealt with in tumuli and
graven ash pits fires still kindling softly
going counter-clockwise in a ceremony long
forgotten why and recitation of feet and meter
lotus-eyed incarnations melodious fragrant
what has been rubbed over with lamp-black
in the south however where the dead migrate
leaving their souls to cling to consonants
often retroflex hard to pronounce and gravid
symbols excised from depths where echo is born
the luminous quantities that count in verse
with a considerable effort of the imagination
divided into ten circles owing to the archaic language
tools to upbraid the demons still on the fringe
heralding battles to come the unconscious
and numinous stupendous clouds rolling
ruddy and billowing from the mouth of Dawn
horse-sacrifice and naming things aloud
ere light first breaks the western shell
what can be mountains and wings or dragons
in myth and tongue of dialects spreading from
their origins in forested hills and dilating
with the intrusion of chariots two-wheeled
in the oriental fray and what is the nature of love
if such be and the four hundred pages turning
to get to the essence her merciful glance

shedding lustrous eons of conflict and does
frame the age of grace sculpted hair from sounds
to be gathered into a mantra and seas that
clamor for their beds and to sleep like that
hidden corpse waters ascending like smoke
altars where it is written finally that fish
and tortoise and other magic emblems
to what avail thunder and lightning the long night
the indelible print of her mouth on the atmospheres
ether and bright the endlessness rim and spokes
of the mind at its source the flow which
proceeds from her lotus-eyes all-merciful

05-12-20

FOOTNOTE TO LOTUS SUTRA

the tongue the mass the hammer the pound
illustrative matter at end follow index
to red line marking not the center but what
is missed at noon when statues listen for
the siren telling them silence has ended
the force the sound the head the loss
fierce zones where syllables don't matter
the words begin then cut-off at the edge
spatial horizons too distant to notice
like mountains hidden in a wing of mist
waterfalls disgorging their secrets in Chinese
to translate exactly what the Buddha said
standing on his makeshift pulpit of bone
the errors in syntax the shifts in tone
paroxysms mistaken for breath and acute
accent the silver beneath the eyelid and deep
inside mercury acting as memory or lunacy
the moon that great ruddy artifact circling
the mind and what is within it enigmas
of punctuation and cellophane sleeping
an engine of imperfect dreams the omphalos
which is at the start and long sequence of rock
of imagination without vowels a fiction borrowed
from clouds and running tacitly beneath
the hexameter an entire hemisphere of water
with holes and the long alarm of light

05-12-20

DIDONE ABBANDONATA

it was a warning without vowels the sinister
greenery climbing the mid-afternoon heat
a horn resounding through the clamped woods
a cave and a muffled siren and clouds
louder than most consonants that end words
a sword play of winds and illicit commerce
among adjectives describing the ethereal musics
the vast panoply of love's armory the neglected
folds and pleats of the surrendered *peplos*
like a figure eight at the feet of the goddess
whose aim is to decrease the number of steps
carved in marble that lead up to the heavens
and people tripping and cumulus thunderheads
driving their invisible horses across a rampant
reddish distance horizon after horizon
opening up to reveal disaster's omniform face
eyes riddled with ant-debris traces of grain offerings
altars spilt over the mosaic floors bon-fires
lit before twilight ascension of smoke alphabets
listening for the mountain to approach with its
phalanxes of headless moors ululating
in long trisyllabic phrases the destiny of dust
powders for the megrims and delicacies at the wrist
perfumed oracular beads systems of skin
rotating in the wild dance of the number three
pivoting on the tip of a Neapolitan song
ankle deep in musk and bare-shouldered
the daring moment of abandonment and
suddenly the black waves the surge on the beach
parasols and trumpets and hip and waist
out of alignment the ships ! caulked and pitched
into the direction where dreams originate
a peninsula of gas and antinomy floating
in the poem's last stanzas strophe after strophe
declining to understand death's mute accent
her hands a flutter of unseen flame and
hair ignited by a single verbal noun
FUOCO ! antiquity goes up in a blaze
statues coruscating with immortality topple
precisely at high-noon and the weave and thump
the hammer and diagonal of eternity

assume masks and ear-rings and bracelets
that refuse to burn even as her soul the size
of a small thrush rises from the incinerator
into the incomplete infinity of the oracle
+ + + + + + + + + + + + + + − + + + + + + + + + + + + + + + + +
you will gather from this account
there are silences greater than sounds
echoes of stone deafening and floral
episodes of fringe and combs
tiny ears shells where seas hide
Neptune himself astride a grain
of sand

05-13-20

PHONETIC DECAY

what is the great news today ?
memory of all things shade and bright
the latest leaf the newest blade of grass
the small conscience peering from behind
the next revolving star the heights and depths
of night and the mouth of dreams and lamps
to wake ? absence and its plenitude
grieving the hour and minute of departure
the unwritten text the missing horoscope
the reading between the lines and the cave
the gaping wound of breath instantaneous
and unresolved as the curtains flutter
and the small crowds of mortals in clumps
gather in a collective effort to Remember
the flames and the ashes the clouds rumbling
in the movie theater and the seas that belong
to the late afternoon when the solar scheme
of things pales fading in an oracular murmur
and the mountain with its dark hegemony
and the lesser hills attributes of myth
the play-acting of the mind and its masks
the you and the me the them and the others
unsettled figures in the palace of mirrors
sweet and sublime the discourse of thought
stone comes into being sand and cliff and
the descending waters and meadows where

foot has never stepped and flowers on display
gorgeous and evanescent like the dew
which gave birth to them and the news is out
that tomorrow will be no better that the raft
and the wing and the apostrophe like
all things of the imagination are not ready
that the vowels scattered throughout the poem
and sounds sybilline and faint and to sleep
in the contours of the archaic consonants
and not to know where the words are
so many deaths and directions
head to the wall and the syntax of distance
like the grammar of silence a code of echoes
what are they ? what are we ?
phonetic decay and nothing more

05-14-20

THE SHORE IS BRIGHT WITH FLAMES

knocked the text out of the blank page
restoring it to river bank and eddying pool
the storm trapped inside a blade of grass
with its dichotomies of speech and light
transgressions of cloud and memory
in a single afternoon capsized face down
in the immersions reflecting the many
who have disappeared traveling south
leaf in hand to the remote dead of the world
a sample of air azure and priceless
the rushing waters of and the glance down
so many precipices in one dream and
to wake between the Om and the Alpha
shedding skin and thought alike a process
of mind relentlessly in pursuit of peace
when the morrow arrives and the flashy
cars that flank the edifices of sorrow
and the statues bidden to step forth speaking
marble interiors of divinity the mansions
floating just inches above earth's surface
inane and invisible and the children at
the doors or peering through windows
asking to have their birthright back and

the arrows that remain stationary high
in the impenetrable sky of planet mercury
bodiless the stations the soul passes through
becoming and then with joy disappearing

05-15-20

LONG DIVISION

perplex and hazard a cloister of stars
racing backwards into the Latin blackboard
spangled spear-flamed illusionary systems
fire-spent and taking any number by five
come up with three the universe a debacle
of child's play in the orient of the imagination
come with me be priceless in devotion
to the wandering bodies of the heavens
dress you up and spin you like a top
the music never stops memory is an elevator
all up and down but nowhere to go
off with you numberless into the great divide
all of space in one hemisphere
and the rest of time in the missing half
so what is there but the burning in the heart
the long tempestuous seas we must cross
the languages of leaf and grass and light
all pervading that numbs the senses
your hand plaited in mine and bedside
sorrows and wondering if ever you'll be back
look up to the plinth and arrow and sob
linking truss to meteor and the flaming inches
between eye and eye will you ever know ?
what separates substance from its lack
the swiftness of mind mistaking distances
comes the towering mountain vast and dark
and the sleepers you and I among them
dreaming it is athwart each bridge we step
rushing wildly the rivers of knowledge
far below and the parameters of syllable
and chisel the statuary rising overnight
precisely where you placed the digit
of your troth and believing forever
is simply another way of saying "die"!

so it goes the daily wreck and routine
the glass of hyperbole and the miasma
which is arriving at noon constantly dazed
the enigma of words always misunderstanding
placing the macron over the wrong vowel
thus flunking the exam and afternoons
tarrying by the broken wall of the pyramid
a song a treble encasement of notes
fluted columns of air and spirals ascending
from the geometry of smoke into
the fabulous unknown of the gods
you one of their chosen fit to pass on
untested by the algebraic equation
a wisp of hair a backward glance
an asterisk lost in the ethereal maze

05-15-20

DAWN ELEGY

*"cuncti adsint meritaeque
expectent praemia palmae"*
Aeneid, V, 70

we keep re-living
the deaths of our loved ones
no getting past that
hands held in the end
that only dissolved
breaths taken no more
pure air and the acid
reality of loss
all goes up in a puff
smoke the intangible language
whatever reaches the welkin
has lost all alphabet can no
more be kenned except in dreams
the sleeper in his fast noose
of mirage and plaint
how does it happen ?
where are they gone ?
to the south to the south
where memory has no force
and the dread life of stone

and distance prevail
do we have recourse to poetry
to recollections of vine and verse ?
intoxicated afternoons dwelling
in a single long cigarette
while phantom bards flit
through glass and tarnish
bidding all an unfinished hour
ash and sputum and hidden violence
the honor of being first in letters
solemn vows to be generous
to acknowledge the superiority
of others as their voices go on
into the frail vowel of night
until the last whisper comes across
through oceans of time
and the stellar sightings one
by painful one in the lawn of sky
a burst of ricocheting asterisks
fire-blooms spraying blazes
the rest is the knowledge
of ending of dust and dusk
dawn imploring day
for one more chance
keep re-living the deaths
of others until the moment
of truth arrives and about
our numbed knees a dark
pall wraps and sends us
plummeting into the void

05-16-20

KYRIE ELEISON

where no rudimentary spire flies his gate
the victor cowed his pride the end has met
down swept winds and toil alike the dead
to compose in their meridian of hap and tide
each a statue of invisibility a shape of ink
of wavering nothingness in the baited light
a swarm of thoughts comes now and then a
dream of mountain slopes of hill and dale
nestling groves and woody tract where myth
its birth retains and still the deaths that mount
steaming steeds that dare the sun to return
his course noon and twilight of each mind
sleeping hard in the ingle of deathless time
so what is now the chaste verbatim of our lore
the depths and iniquities that mark each losing
day the slights and ire that register in the courts
appeals to a higher sound to an echo rising above
its common vowel a speech act clad in marble
heard by one small leaf alone as trembling it
shakes off its memory off like dew and vanishing
its voice a sad plaint gone lost in substances of steam
like clouds unworried as they scud the lofty zones
terrains by gods abandoned losses and mourning
that we alone can count our own with grief
the numberless by now spiked and sparked like
asterisks blown from the furnaces of oblivion

05-17-20

ON A BRIGHT MORNING IN MAY THE ACHAEANS GATHER ON THE BEACH PREPARED TO SET FORTH INTO GLORY TAKING WITH THEM LITTLE BROTHER

let me O muses struggle to remember
hard by the dry well and the rocky hillside
who they were among the many displayed
banners fluttering in the morning breezes
they were the countless as pebbles arrayed
and we sent little brother forth among them

and the multiple fires and ash the altars fuming
and how many skies as well elaborate and fine
dawning azure like Chinese silks around their
sleeping heads wrapped dreaming the day
set sail they would and fixtures in their minds
going on and off and their eyes open yet not
seeing who they were girding their belt-zones
feeling in the dark for the hafts of their swords
and how many boats black and hollow they
were assembled on the sandy dunes and mirages
of distant mountains like glories of victory
and insane charges of horses in the black
the fray of cuff and hem and sleeve and buckler
the gnashing of teeth waking from one sleep
only to fall into the next taking little brother
with and unable to read the signs on high who
they were shining and not shining pitched in
the eerie pre-dawn murk and behind them
countries vast and wooded and the sounds
and echoes of the fathers long drowned like
eels in the muddy pools and ponds of memory
each arm raised to greet some invisible god
or other the plenitude of tongues murmurs
threats and moans the priceless moment of love
bidding farewell to hearth and wife and kids
slumbering in their maze and who they were
could I recount each and every including in
their midst little brother of the wan smile
for whom no other sun would shine and great
agitation and motion like planets unknown coming
into sight gathering half dead already on the shore
would clamber and elbow their ways on board
muttering half-recalled prayers words eaten off
in the middle syllables like quoits flung into the blue
vowels recanting and consonants in the middle
jungles of orbits in their brains forgetting their
own names a bustle of contradictions human and
medley of gods weaving half-heartedly in between
taking little brother by the hand and hoisting him
up on the planks the enormous sea wafting danger
and hypothesis in the early glare shrieks of sea-fowl
wings flapping wildly against the sun's chargers
and what more were they but minions of thought

creatures of parable and fable weaklings tormented
like statues by the notion of *being* a riot of the senses
demented in the excess of lust and prevarication
rueful admonitions of conscience if I could but
O muses name each one but so many the decades
that have rolled over my briny head so few the days
bright and actual that I have lived in the swarming
and left to idle by the broken dock watching the swill
come up to my knees to fret over distances of their
faces pale and fade in the tremendous jostling
who they could ever have been acting masks in
a pivot of earth-tremors little brother lost in
the shuffle of rumor and demand salt and sand
mists of flight into the arcana of the heavens
myth and footnote details erased by the thumb of time
fate-stricken whoever they were I cannot name
the more I struggle leaves that rustle whispers
but nothing more comes back of the ink spent
transliterating whatever it was the muses sang

05-18-20

THE HYMN TO PERSEPHONE

joy and bitterness great I greet Thee
both and sorrow the plaint and murmur
do then shed on us luster for another day
and moments when lost in the bazaar
of reflections we too forget the living self
and which direction take and veer off
course as usual in memories when others
did with us play and plight the unforgotten
weave the sections of air the cloud-warp
rushing the swift wing of light to its end
to Thee then I plead altars of floral display
embroidery of Italian vowels the bright
and high afternoon ahead and joined in
hands of thought let us wander to the hills
where dialect of sun and meandering myth
create noble error the fiefdom of mind
absence and finally thrust us from motion
into the still plenitude of silence Thou
who in dress of blooming hues Primavera

shine as rays of holy planet before returning
beneath to skull-king Pluto Thy groom
and us bereft above on sullen fields of earth
forsaken another day to mend and sleep

05-18-20

ETERNITY RECONSIDERED

hills where dialects are born
from the brow of myth full-blown
brush and foam dyes and tinctures
of sound echoing vales and leaves
the airs resound becoming green
a distance of verdant hues if only
childhood had not lapsed and paths
once trod daily but faint markings
on earth's corrugated surface
and what is left to say and decry
but absences & intermittent silence
what numbers left undone what letters
left lingering in mid-air fingered
by invisible hands as if sleeping
their interminable vowel of memory
shapes and tombs and underneath
the serpent head the crafted idol
bronze and gold-fringed offering
to a deity who remains faceless
the warrant of another life to come
despair at the root in the slopes
and groves where padded whispers
footprints in the winds small curls
and arabesques of a secret oracle
and do islands still resist and cliffs
and promontories that jut out far
into the undisciplined atmospheres
of ruin and grief and is this the one
and only chance to reverse the mask
parading as statues do in their hiatus
of aphasia the persons of the dream
warring with consonants dense and
irreverent dim and thundering if
and always if quickening breath

could revive the ones we've lost
meandering in the cities of the plain
remote beings vanished entities
bodies once talking shadows
now transformed leaves darkening
in the brief syllable of time

05-19-20

THE COCKTAIL PARTY

"caos: no tiene plural"
    Carlos Fuentes

set out the folding chairs on the north lawn
and let the living be seated on them
whatever their ages give them large-print folios
so they can follow the recitation easier
the Latin word order will work itself out
the syllables will fall into place tone and accent
and by hour's end Latin will turn into Italian
with the irksome quarrels between Orlando and Rinaldo
whose identities never stay the same and
be sure they are replenished with drinks and canapés
their looks are glazed and famished
so much to discuss before twilight
tell me again which dynasty is this
the last but one , *Sir*
they say there is a *Specter* at the door
let the porter usher him to the side porch
where the screens and fireflies are
who would name their daughter *Persephone* ?
so much etymology remains obscure
the sounds are narrower and the diphthongs
with annoying frequency in the scansion
you can distinguish the Trojans from the Argives
as their cries are like those of birds hoopoes or cranes
at dawn rushing to escape the winter storms
and the ruddy insect climbing the bamboo stalk
and that *thing* with almost human eyes biding
by the wall-tapestry and the connections between
the guests who come late with the earlier ones
difficult to discern between the living and the dead
who should be directed to the south lawn

where there is the echoing of the names of Shiva
all thousand and eight pronounced in heroic meter
do they call those priests *bonzes* ?
saffron orange and ocher their robes in tatters
and yes begging bowls and muttering mantras
please let us back to the *House*
but as to who can enter it and who can exit
who knows unless it is by the cut of their shadows
and *that* presence with tawny eyes and a sheet of flame
there is no clear direction the loudness
and bright of the wind instruments and
the pedal organ and harmonium all at once
what is the cause of this celebration ?
the Muses nine in their catastrophic outfits
dancing and singing on the cut grass and
the clear air and the planets already visible
though the sun is still driving his beasts
into the mountain it is a matter of mortality
of bringing to a close this chapter of life
and those who do not require help breathing
take those machines away and those
who have already passed into the beyond
eclipsed asterisks memories lopped off at the helm
hands still on swords and falling by the wayside
or into poorly improvised ditches and dogs
and birds-of-prey at them all raucous
who was that *Specter* at the door ?
come nightfall who will recall the who the where
the why so much distraction and the painted air
the voluble heightened clouds lowering
gussets and frills and the prayers offered
to the One-Who-Burns-in-the-Sea
what is a photo-glyph and who can count
the signs flashing in the atmospheres ?

05-20-20

THE ANTIQUITIES !

ablaze the Punic skies of morning !
the goddesses in their quicksilver cothurns
astride their celestial bicycles their dawn-gowns
ravaged by the magnetic winds of grammar
hair flaming carmine and crimson unkempt
seducing the tiny gods of the Olympian lintel
kisses burning into the airs and clouds
unwrapped defamed and tossed aside
O beauties of Quintessence ! clamor for more !
desire the unquenchable mortals who lie
languishing in stables punished for their
inability to conjugate the irregular *verbs* !
would that children could grow up and suffer
and be savage in all the lineaments of divinity
that earth with its truculent seas and waxen mountain-tops
furnaces and refrigerated cars would turn
ever faster at dizzying speeds of light
the destinies of Zeus and Mercury compounded
in the dram of salt it takes to dissolve Memory !
for why do we wake daily and take these lessons
to heart and full of remembrance and nostalgia
meander to the wells to fill our jugs with
the nectar of poesy ? whatever we learn to read
to recite to put to mind the clashes and quizzes
of so many heroes and centaurs at the man-root
of passion and then what ? we grow old
wizened mnemonic factors in the legends
of the antiquities rocks and minerals and lesions
sparkling veins in the stone fragments statues
leaning on Zephyrus blowing their cheeks out
and dead all but dead in the living recall
of the Nymphs out to sun their immortal skins
on the flashing river-side and murmuring quartos
of illegible verse the denizens of Thought !
does One day simply become another ?
tomorrow when the Island comes to dock
by the temple of Minerva and the rioting of
bards vying with the photographs of Apollo
and all the noise of Rumor winging chaotically
in the Egypt of Time ! what then of the class
where distinctions on the Map are reduced

to a set of vowels to be memorized by night
and the ignition of dreams in the outlines
of the streaming goddess the unwholesome
with faces painted loud as the cinema of Infinity !
it is forever in the Now of yesterday and all
events are capsized in the thumbnail sketch
of the Archaic and beautiful and resounding
in the ear of Echo the interminable !
Aurora fleeing the night-stalls of Script
to burst like dew only to vanish in the newest
Antiquity of all : *Chaos !*

05-20-20

WHITE-ARMED HELEN

so spoke Iris fleet of foot to Helen
at the loom come look to see which
of the two will deserve to call you
dear wife the troubled fares and fates
of mankind the wars and tribulations
passion-fueled that kindle strife and ire
hands aloft to wrathful Mars his palms
directing cloud and thunder the bolts
that reduce to ash the theaters of men
and cliff and hillside where dwell sweet
shepherds and nymphs in bucolic hour
what of the rest of history to come ?
at the window stares out to watch
the dueling pair was ever woman so
fraught with duality the winter-storms
of mind the thought-fret of mortality
whence the gods in their plenitude
of lies wrath and duplicities she foams
raising her glass to empty folds and words
recondite and half-lost in their syllabic
nonsense prayers and oaths uttered
between her flashing teeth vowels
escaped into the oblivion of eternity
and consonants ruptured at the middle
like seas of ruddy distance and mountains
painted to resemble in lasting peace
the obdurate porphyry of false promises

she bares a shoulder to sense the rays
the sun's last warmth of a passing day
slants the asterisk against the pane
shifting threads between red and gold
the tongue gone dry harsh breath
from a convulsed throat which of the two
she wonders maimed at the heart by truth
that she is victim of an unspun destiny
like colors shattered in the eastern winds
and deep below in the down-spread vale
her gaze on the path that leads to hell
her softest inner despises its own self
a shadow she begins to float to other
climes where Pharaoh and Sphinx part
time into unequal hemispheres and
her name resounds hollow the echo
of a leaf bedewed in remote antiquity

05-21-20

ADOLESCENCE

what was I thinking when I first put
word to paper and let ink spread its
slow drawl into spirals and curlicues
moon-letters whiter than incandescence
and pyres that lit the brain and stained
left-wise and right the surrounding air
billows of thought-clouds irises and
fireflies the adjectives tumbled forth
beside nouns just come into being and
no syntax guided the rays of vowels
but led astray whatever reason left
behind and finger by finger the grasses
of my lexicon spread far and wide
the disease of empty prosody until full
bloom the designations for other worlds
for myths and echoes of lingering antiquity
rock and fold the deepest incline toward
hell's unique entrance near the gasoline
pump that stands alone between planets
that have yet to start their course and
how was it I turned the page and multiplied

to excess the entries to a paradise of sky
fast rushing through itself to become
even more heaven on the other side and
what ! I exclaimed to my other self brother
in repair of time look how much the hues
taint the unspoken sound and brighter
yet the sun before it even rises splendor
in sleep to behold and greater heights
climb like vine or ivy on the stucco wall
dividing the perils of imagination from
its own chaos and faint I heard the first
resound of a finished *poem* the likes of
which I must now bury in sweet oblivion

05-21-20

DREAM SPELL I.

formal delivery storm and billowing word
effects the nominal division of sleep and space
categories floral and mountainous at once
the steep descent and following creatures
into the place where vowels or are we between
spades and decks ? flashing images of pop
stars in the raw and hats and gloves and
prophylactics by night and the advent
of a lunar calendar based on Mayan pro-
vectives and the sprawl and dialect of verse
in its various hagiographies the delectation
to ruin and above all homophones of the sun
verging on aphasia lunacy and verbatim
transcripts of owl-speech the dominant tone
yellow-eyed of the goddess Minerva in her
guise as the Hag-of-the-Crossroads and so
much we owe to Hesiod in his perplexity
of the births and minimalizations of gods
speeding like quicksilver through the fringe
based on window-display and target practice
anomalous subscript iota and hexameter
flushed and scanned in photographic dots
almost a painting in reverse with hues and
abstracts of grass and the mower of pages
directed at meridian the semblance of

memory with its first and second brides
in empress bee-hive hair-do humming sotto
voce the arias of Monteverdi opera dark
as the deathless channels of oblivion set
to music and what a lark the radio and its
new manifestations walkie-talkie wrist-watch
hello ! can you hear me ? mummy and dolphin
decorative assertions of the third Dynasty
when sand came into being and sky at
once the novel of the marriage between kids
snatched from their hive of luxury and sent
yes into the ionosphere a movie in sepia
about the origins of thought and cosmos
and Bang ! interpretations in the Mayo clinic
a void of x-rays and cast off paper schemes
walking sadly home when drugs have run
their course and you feel divine but for
what ? next to you walking cadaver
named Brother and the gasoline station
abandoned by the deities and twilight ever
darkening the leaves and the stars

05-22-20

DREAM SPELL II.

she said her name was *Bavarian Honeysuckle*
the path was littered with dead pine-cones and
dandelions in profusion to bend down and
take the humus in deep breaths a dizzying sleep
of the organism and evolving skies penetrating
the back-brain in cups of depth and sheer in-
toxication as she lifted her skirts knee high and
sang as do cicadas every 17 years adolescent
that she was in pinafore and migraine a long
avenue behind her which no camera could reach
catching in chiaroscuro the relief of being human
between the shoulders and trying to keep her
in sight the modulating atmospheres of classics
the periphery where the eye no longer can and
finally intuiting the music in her being tick-tock
and dot dot dot refrain of radiophonic madness
she winked she laughed she bounced and played

jacks on the sidewalk and looking up just once
clouds swarmed her eyes and dimpled smile
all maze and refraction of light in water dazzle
dragonflies flitted in and out and the margin
swelled with honey-colored air were we to
invite a swim in the nearby freshet disposing
of skin and asterisk and diving down into
the narcissistic bottoms the exchange of hands
and identical as twins the both of us ethereal
bodiless the formation of geminated consonants
set like wet pearls between vowels coruscating
as suns in the twelfth night of summer what a !
and what else could be discerned coming up for
a swipe of clean air and the pond-scum green
and evanescent fingers of bright and on the bank
where we tossed our clothes now a glowing ossuary
such as mortals leave behind in the great decay

05-22-20

PRIAM

I have traveled to Phrygia rich in vines
men god-like and skilled in horse taming
wrapped in cones of dust with feathers
painted the hues of an untenanted sky
effusions of powder cinnabar saffron
the very oils that anoint kings and in
my dilapidated car toured hillsides and
turrets high with beacons and pennons
and listened for hours as bards related
origin-myths of seas and nymphs born
to lure mortals to their end and on a rock
jutting forth into day sat entranced seeing
myself in other lives youthful again a flirt
with naiads in their liquid haunts and
to the woods where I could sport with music
calling the clouds by their rightful names
in other lives too where I wended a seer
with threads unraveling in chambers dark
or straddling cushions on ancient porches
waiting for new planets to emerge wet
with a mysterious luster and slept deep

within stone and spoke in other tongues
to the great and mighty dead of holy *Verse*
who introduced me in echoes and italics
to endless souls their lament and plaint
of becoming bodies that cast shadows
how in another life could I endure these
matters sleeping in rife and reckless way
driving my car blind through rains lasting
forty years and to return if there was
such a road directing me to southland
nothing but a cemetery and a waste
where leaves employ the speech of men
assuming selves that weep all night
could I but wake and simply walk across
kingdoms that last a day and no more
were I nothing but a hieroglyph a mote
glancing through the air of dusky Phrygia
again a dreamer in the eroded hills
asking for silence of the weeping leaves
souls of men intaglios of the *Invisible*
all my sons and Hector too !

05-23-20

THE SIBYL'S MOUTH

there as far as a spear can fly
resides the eye and all it sees
encompassed in a single thought
unburdened weight the light
aspired by all that wake and
living walk through portals
dark the quest for a magic key
to unlock such nights as seize
the wandering mind asleep in
its days of unnumbered time
that's as far as it can go the spear
far-flung the dank and western hill
to sleep where one can never wake
but aspire to lunacy moon-drunk
laurels curving about the brow
temples each to a goddess spelled
how can fifty-two be a number ?

what do they call the one who
lives unseen in garden furrows ?
and the one who resides at the top
of the stairs smoking cigarettes ?
beware their language-maze
tongue-tied vowels in excess
the panoply of retroflex consonants
geminates and diphthongs and
highest of the bright a syllable
beyond control sonic and terminal
both in velocity and quiescence
long for me ! they cry convulsed
phrases uttered in mid-speech
like statues or gargoyles spouting
ancient seas of smoke and dust
or antiquity in the *sibyl's mouth*
oracle enigma and depth-charge
dazzle and chronic waste of light
to rewire the ear and the hives
where winter terminates its oaths
long for me ! like kestrels mewing
through clouds and intricacies of air
saint and spoor and disappearing ink
fingers that learn to fly released
of their debt to grass and chasms
where unsuspecting children
are reborn as sigma tau or psi
how can fifty-two be a number ?
what is hap and circumstance
and what is memory other than
the world beneath the thumbnail's
darkening cathedrals ?

05-24-20

GNOMIC VERSE

what will the butterfly catch
or the grasshopper in long grass
what will the moth of bended wing
or the mile of ants in the Cyclops' eye ?
such summer as it was with *Mary Lou*
fields of corn heaped to the sky
relentless months perspired at noon
heaven lowered its bickering clouds
and thunder rent the town in two
the bridge and river and trees
that accompany the final melody
the vistas from the water-tower
or the hospital hove into view
the stars to reach a single night
and fill the porch with fire-fly light
gone it was summer with *Mary Lou*
hasp and buckle and tarnish of the gods
foot-steps on soft lunar turf
elbow and shoulder of mythology
the great religions of mankind
a simple mark left on the dreaming mind
when school is out and twine undone
the labyrinth of Crete the crumbled vowels
of Minoan script and whatever else
a diploma holds the child is done
the learning gone and dust askew
summer with *Mary Lou* no more
winter's crabbed grasp frost and hoar
the glass reduced to dark night
each finger a hand gone wrong
distance forever in the myriad eye
and sleep the dense inch
dead insects ply

05-24-20

TO UNDERSTAND POETRY

*"E' gli diceva di sua crudel sorte
e come andava cercando la morte"*
Pulci, Morgante, XXII, 190

I am still roaming the south hills
briars and brambles heat and insects
buzzing skies torment of August to come
thunderhead and purple roaring engines
invisible to steal from love its fruits
over-ripe and now distant dusky
grasses grow there no more and
the verses sown in the dense furrows
speak in italics to the ghosts
who keep asserting there is no after-life
and *her* I see and *him* too and others
who clinging to the raft of stone
drugged with light soon vanished
marking the advent of the photograph
that captures shadows and backgrounds
of tree and marble epitaph and walking
slowly back to homes that exist no more
signaling to clouds above to burst
and let rains fall and wash the soils away
the unmarked paths the riverbanks
what brain can retain so many scenes
the rapid passage of chiaroscuro dreams
hands that yield and fingers lost in
the heavens rolling high and the theater
of mind trying to adjust three and three
the number it takes to forget some say
and what is to understand of protests
in the streets and wars of far-off lands
the gone who remain nameless but for
the occasional song the vehement sound-
recording of their whittled voices like
initials carved on bark denoting love's
eternal knot and all the paraphernalia
of learning and the abscess of thought
and cumulating syllogisms denying truth
in the faltering airs we breathe and I
still wandering on the southern hill
pacing through a dense wood to

discern *what* in the dwindling dusk
a comet bearing my *Beatrice* her
brown rings of hair now indistinct
poetry to dwell on *this* and oblivion
the best part of her unreal self
contours devil-dust swirling in the eye
how dark the cavern of memory swells
the end is here the end that has always been
death and only death is in the kiss
sealed by summer's circulating heat
and to lie there for a moment guessing
which star will be the first to appear
in the abandoned atmospheres
and sleep always now in the nettled brush
where leaf follows leaf green murmuring
then disappears in one last unheard note

05-25-20

MEMORIAL DAY 2020

for my uncle Vernon MIA ca. 1945

look at the wee wriggling creatures
I see writhing in the grasses souls
my dear of the lamented ones who
departed before their time what sprites
squeaking in their devilish tongues of yore
their missing sight and deaf forever
sundered from the pounding of the drum
would they had mouths to speak the many
of all the suffering and useless gore
the wars that employed them like clouds
of insects and poisoned snakes abound
rock and mire stone and bluff the heights
and landscapes in verses once told and
chants of distant choirs a blare of horns
trumpets of jazz angels gone blank
like a reverie of wounded bats or Lucifers
multiple in their chasm of fell pride
how furious the soils they turn rounding
nights eternal and nevermore a cry
ripped from each leaf and torn from roots
deep underground the colorless blood

of ancient gods and thrones too I guess
carved from human bone and array of planes
zooming in an archaic sky like hummingbirds
without eyes and bodies riddled with hematite
come look no more and let us to the parade
it's glory-day the memorial of unremembered
joys and the floundering of nations
dumbfounded rulers regents and the like
in bullet proof cars speeding now afar
from these hallowed lawns of time
look no more let these grasses teem
with their extinct fireflies and parachutes
the world's a loss and nothing gained
to step so gingerly among the living dead
'tis you and I the next to go
so with hushed mind march on through
dew and mist ecstatic errors of the self
like moving shadows on a Chinese screen

05-25-20

THE ROAD NOT TAKEN

the past : a shadow of grasses
wind and unseen lamps glimmering
the past : a finger a tumulus buried
figure-eights in a small garden plot
the past : a voice issuing from a mirror
darkened glass reflecting back no more
the past : lying on our backs endless
summer night counting stars
the past : green everywhere the path
winding back through fossil trees
the past : silence

like the time driving through the dust
an angel black as night landed on the car hood
metal turned to instant flame our amaze
eyes dilated watching the great azure wings
go up in a vapor and a voice calmly
urging us to quit the body
what with four ships burnt behind us
and Italy still left to be discovered
the potent vowels the hurried consonants

of the unbidden oracle how we hastened
to understand and yet could not turn the wheel
steering our destinies through song and mud
what ! July was soon upon us and
a jazz solo saxophone sounding in the leaves
a whisper of time and then surrender !

we learned about art and the principles of
line and structure and bent our faces
forward into the light and discerned shapes
lunar and cavities of the sun and the sound
of horses racing through the invisible afternoon
by the roadside couples turned to watch
the glazed sky slowly collapse turning
the world into unending twilight
one by one we separated unknowingly
the car was left abandoned in a ditch
some call the City of Angels

the past : the road not taken

05-26-20

GOING STEADY

I waited and waited and waited
for her to return
to give some sign a wave
of her small white hand
or the comb in her hair
and the burnish of the sun
as she as she as she
or in the snowy moonlight
in a fairy-tale sleigh ride
breath cold as ice forming shapes
in the air in the air as she as she
through the corn fields baking
in the terrific August sun August sun
as she in the fairy sleigh a cloud
her mouth or the comb she took
slowly unwinding each vowel
for her to return
but she is a ghost in a nascent mall
looking into each plate glass window

for a gift to give me to give me
a small white hand waving or
a book no one can read
a forgery of life a windmill
small as the luster in her eye
when she takes the comb out of
out of her hair out of
to return to return I am waiting
promised to save a dance
in plate-glass window
a ghost in a new shopping mall
and the dead who keep going back
looking for something they know not
what ! she is in the baking August sun
an angel turned to soot
and raving and raving and raving
this is memory waiting
on a small brown hill
below the water tower
by the apple orchard where the terraces
slope repeatedly into their hospital
who is *that* ?
I am grown up today and the photo
no longer exists that shows her
that shows her that shows her
as she was
grown up today and I am I am
waiting to die

05-26-20

AT THE COURT OF AUGUSTUS

sea and sky confused mixed the elements
wheel spokes of the sun in disarray
Neptune his hoary sea-girt head opposes
rising and shaking air imbued and roaring
with terrifying squalls the swelling azure
burst and flotsam of archaic shipwreck
so as advertised the epic tempestuous sight
in cine-color verbatim action shots under
water floating naiads with shell-fused hair
will love make them stronger will driving

winds turned submarine-green at velocities
no skin withstands and the paraphernalia
of the gods in bright necklaces ear-rings
the size of distance and eyes enormous
with envy and design attributes of the poem
at large the weaponry skilled at perfection
and shorelines where wasted damsels and
the next of kin breathlessly watch the joust
of triremes on fluttering canvas drained of
blood the mariners with superhuman titles
plunge uselessly into the salty wastes and cries
like gulls wheeling wounded overhead and
the lattice-work of clouds blooming porphyry
in the maze of atmospheres drilled and white
with aftershock and a whistle so shrill it
cannot be heard recalling the troops home
the grizzled navvies adorned with Mycenenan
names the role of king a pointless designation
down to the hull to plug the leaks and wails
and omens and portents the dozens of birds
of varying hue prepared to dive into the feast
arm and limb and sinking armor-plate vast
and ineffable the sinking mortal husks who
will lament the unknown what brides will
never sense the juxtaposed fleshy pulse
a blind inaction of the divinities a panorama
bleak and remote as the mountains painted
on the western cusp and the words countless
and disordered in fragments on the pasted
remnants of an immense and unforged myth
the who and where and why and in untitled
cantos the hooting and going under timbers
of rotten pine and pitch the vertigo of mind
caught in the swirl of liquid dreams hands
that beg for air and the crystalline deaths
both beautiful and terrible in the improvised
sun-down of the poet's last recitation

05-27-20

AD FAUCES GRAVE OLENTIS AVERNI

the dance the ligatures the phonetics
the great combine of astral projections
mythology of rock and hagiography of stone
theogony of the multiple grasses underfoot
personifications of cloud and mist calling
back and forth between the relentless hours
of the single day in time when we are bidden
to come forth in raiment of sleep and sand
and the bursts of purple blooms in skies
racing and minute caught in a reflecting
glass the underside of deities intended
to last the length of ink and the thousands
of other gods each with an inch of silk
for mind and how does it all work which
is the way out of the flower's dense dream
of light and which the way back to hills
shaped like the flood of thoughts from
the orient the ear and the basilisk and
the totem seer carved from mountain pine
cool evenings that cannot last and fireflies
lit for an hour only in the porch of reveries
confound dreamers with their black flocks
and mountain paths and dusky groves
where shades of the dearly departed linger

what is that to us excavating the airs
for some sign to guide us toward doors
that yawning open will let us recognize
who we have been and then to dissolve
in fleeting colors that embroider the sun's
great eye and what of the seas within pink
shells with their boom and echo of salts
the tongues that prattle on about births
and deaths of languages and their rites
vowels in glassy clusters and harmonies
and consonants fixed like stars in darkness
what are we but statues half alive at noon-bright
pleading from dumbfounded pedestals
for the instant of immortality promised
when first the light of day was born
I was a only a child! the grievous plaint
that marks each being with humanity

the up and down episodes of smoke and
futility the emptied heavens and vast
and what of the tiny signatures in grass
wings ! the multifaceted eye of the soul
dwelling in the tenuous hive of echoes
if only ! if only ! and the leaf turning on its
syllable of memory slowly darkening
in night's unyielding embrace

05-28-20

AULA MAGNA

*"Ibant obscuri sola sub nocte per umbram
perque domos Ditis vacuas et inania regna"
Aeneid, VI, 268-269*

obscure persons on a solitary night through
shadow and empty realms and vacant houses
the under-thought of breath the everlasting
dark where Persephone in floral raiment
dreams of the *New Season* of troubadours
and the mulberry leaf spreading verdure
like a prayer to the unremembering sky
to forget is ever the choice of the dead
and the rusted gate hanging by one hinge
trying to say it in Italian come nightfall
recalling umbrellas and spouts and convex
centers of the passing heavens and glories
that never were but words inflected loud in
a hollow classroom the *Aula Magna* where
ghosts of students crib their knowledge
of archaic tongues hurried hieroglyphs
that cling to obscure sounds haunted vowels
hiatus and despair unable to locate the echo
of a pronoun long since disappeared
night skies alone and a hand searching for
its other a diapason of unheard music fingers
tangled in reeds and crumbling rock and
persons marked for *no-return* in somber
chasms corridors winding this way and that
why didn't they read the grammar-book ?
what was the rule-of-thumb for memory ?
fatal moments in the history of western thought

when stone was set up over cloud and consonant
now *Pluto* sits alone in the warehouse of sleep
raveling and unraveling what little he knows
about the *mind* confusing it with the lattice
of wing and distance yellowing in the eyes
of child-bride Persephone the *obscure*
who sees and does not see the passengers
disembarking from Charon's weightless boat
cannot look back to the lapsing shore of light
remote and fast recall of the ancient time
when a small ringing bell ended the lesson
of memorized paradigms and planetary spells
vanishing voices of leaves that cried
        centum errant annos

05-29-20

CORONA VIRUS SUTRA

besieged aggrieved the world at a loss
nowhere to turn the hospitals the alcoves
the paramedics the Filipino nurses in the ICU
the ambulance drivers the rippling floors
the termites in the walls and mosquitoes
breeding diseases the distances between
man and man the irreconcilable remoteness
of the emotions one from the other the brain
finding excuses not to be rational to exclude
love from the equation the nation at large
a political debacle sick with respiratory distress
choked by atmospheric pollution and cops
the mountains hands-off and the meadows of
paradise a small snatch of literature shepherds
disguised as courtiers or vice versa glosses
for words gone out of style lexicons of death
synonyms and homophones for rival black
suns that orbit man's wayward dream
hypotenuse and equator endlessly burning
chronologies of the plague and legends
of the year *thirteen hundred* which is *today*
and the photographs in oil and vitriol of
one thousand and eight fish belly-up flashing
silver in the laconic late afternoon lake

x-ray and thumbprint of those testing
positive for their humanity and excesses
of vowel in the enigmatic and aphasic
poetries mailed daily to the editorial board
whosoever judges by the gun and *et cetera*
mouths gasp for consonants and syllabic laws
to justify another day on this mirage wobbling
into the ozone strangling on its own core
Gaia! moonshine and mendacity at large
wheels a-spinning the eternal verities like
smoke signals sent to red planet Mars
cacophony of sirens science fiction UFOs
dot and squiggle of the Holy See and asterisks
representing the dregs of mankind sent into space
circularity of religion and reason death-trap
of language similitude and opposition sound-bites
how has "at last" become this very instant ?
mask and glove supermarket and prayer-wheel
dust to dust the great ocher Eye gone blind
western occlusion systems oriental Zed
scientology and Hare Krishna on the Steps
the dance of phonetic decay ! illusionism
body bags unmarked graves and disbelief
do you hear what I hear ?

05-30-20

THE HIGH HOLY DAYS

"quae lucis miseris tam dira cupido?"
Aeneid, VI, 721

imagine the time when the opening lines
of the Rg Veda were constructed
clarified butter and syllables praising
the fire god *Agni* words not written
but uttered by inspiration
rock and grass sky and cloud
emanations of a hidden divinity
the holy and sanctified were everywhere
consecrated by ritual and
what is today but a brief interlude
warring sides as if Detroit and Cincinnati
had to choose or the Pope and Naples

would divide America between themselves
George Floyd ! peaceful protesters gather
before the Palace anger not ritual makes
holy the tensions in the diseased atmosphere
burning cars as if Arjuna himself wild
with the death of his son were running amok
a thousand arrows at a time sent from his Bow
or jackal crow and dog sniffing blood-soaked earth
and the hundreds of slain and headless
mushrooming in a deserted parking lot
police protection a myth lies of democracy
tales of the rebirths of the Buddha
near holy Varanasi a thousand epochs ago
folk-lore of talking animals wily plotting
to take over city-states and dust in orbs
rolling from the saddened hills and cries of
George Floyd ! threaten the body politic
grim trial of breath and cameras going viral
amazing grace Aretha Franklin ! question
the soul of man ! in a tumble-down shack
where the minister of Fate resides
counting the fingers remaining to him
was light ever sweeter on the slope ?
did bees in such swarms descend from myth
to consecrate the empress's hair-do ?
over one hundred five thousand dead now
hospitals vomit the corpses and
a Boddhisattva reborn as an ambulance driver
counts the number of patients remaining
and in the height of the sixteenth century
Giorgio Vasari publishes the Lives of the Artists
from Cimabue to Michelangelo
and the Pope and Naples plot to divide Italy
and the Book of the Courtier and Arcadia
et cetera in the fabric of history tawdry
excesses of ambition and power
in counterpoint with the mind's passion to sing
which is it the sublime voices of a Palestrina mass
or the architecture of Mozart's Haffner symphony ?
pull the plug on the American Experiment
Jefferson and Washington slave-holders
cradle of liberty a venture capitalist scheme
George Floyd ! the high holy days are upon us

sirens police dogs tear-gas shells looting
turn the streets upside down inside out
immigrant small business owners crying
inequalities of wealth and property distribution
lunatic abacus rigged elections bankruptcy
and The President flying to his Private Golf
somewhere near crocodile infested Everglades
burning the opening lines of the Rg Veda
scorching the clarified butter and
vowel and consonant so carefully placed
ransacked the tombstones of the gods !
are there still angels ready to plummet
like exhausted comets to the cities of man ?
Burn Baby Burn ! Marvin Gaye where are you ?
a tiny Buddha misplaced among plastic toys
in a Brooklyn bargain basement
what can he do and to what avail ?
George Floyd ! mama mama
prostitutes in black face in the White House
information overload tweeted to death
the disciples of the former Jesus Christ
in Maoist garb storming the New York Public Library
pillage and loot and plunder and torch !
Venice is flooded and the Pope is helpless
ringing and ringing the Fixed Star called *Nemesis*
the high holy days are long upon us and
we struggle to breathe only to breathe
as free men on a free planet
George Floyd ! mama mama

05-31-20

THE BERLITZ METHOD

it doesn't make for good poetry
to dwell on the moment to count the hands
on either arm the fingers crawling in the grass
to recount over and over the front lawn
and the porch and the rocking settee and
how evenings turned into bad lyrics with a
fling of fireflies and the first time the girls
put lipstick on and the car motor ever a mystery
in the night making for flawed subject matter
you turned to me and I looked away
listening to the distant boom and flare
of police weaponry someone's on fire again
the building's only made of paper the moon
has nothing to do with it just the tide pull
and the account of one who drowned
or was he yanked under the truck wheels
one long Greek afternoon and the grammar
book of replies and to learn a new syllabary
recalling the map and the structure of names
in the index and the little figure drawings
representing a god withholding gifts
even as the sea pulls itself up large and shining
gold glints on each menacing wave
not the best time for poesy and its syntax
a lexicon of archaicisms rock fragments
with mental inscriptions the slow decay
of morphology and strings of unknown
consonants or backwards looking letters
an entire mirror of efforts to appear at *being*
the enigmatic unfolding from its envelope
and becoming the poem of the moment

05-31-20

VESTIGES OF A SOLITARY MIND

strictly latin speaking the thought
a mind occurs to have sinking process
depths sundered a wilderness of light
inextricable moments in the hive where
happening and cancellation occur
the often as not doubt and negation
going forward alone branch in hand
to dispel fears and approach the Gate
as one who has only half-learned
the paradigm shadow wandering lost
in the woods to listen intently to the leaf
in the umbratile moment when echo
takes the wind for its own shivering
in the cause and effect of memory
as if to inform but only hints accidents
then rush falling a stumble against
the fragment and suddenly vowels
bright in the ear loosen meaning from
its axis stupefied look around the world
shaped now like water in a waist of
denial the shoulders looming in sleep
their own weight the collapse of systems
to be loud and answer to no one ! so
it seems the vacuum has its lexicon
of asterisks and despair lighting brief
and fierce the western sheet of sky
as it begins burning at the far corner
a reminder that day's end is spread out
already on the south lawn where gather
puerperal and dazed the newly dead
who yielded to a single finger folding
as only you can also the origami and
puzzle of distance each a mountain and
longing phased in syllables dense and dusk
at last the self-same woods bewildered
shifts in time the waking no better
than the loss of consciousness if only
tomorrow the troth and fling of air
space and its tremendous redundancy
where is to go if not inward to the seed
of light and language both returning

the unsaid to its empty clause figuring
there is no higher number no poorer
soul in its plight of person and mask

06-01-20

PENTIMENTO

a clue an illusion the heels
taken to the dust in corollas of fake suns
the blackening unit of space no longer
than no broader than the thumb's span
we are poor to notice the reflecting pool
with its faces borrowed from the moon
and lay aside armor and nettles
fruiting branches that wither
in our hands ever as the sky's molten
crescent scorches angels in flight
the task is not communion but division
in the round-about of a false sleep
deep in the ingles of the forbidden wood
where light is the briefest dream

broken the bodies of the hemispheres
each a half and more and stained
the color of rock after it has been excised
from matter and the howls and cries
what of their length like ink
trailing into the moon's wake
on a starless night and we mortals
heart-struck and bent on a narcissistic
path to our own destruction immured
in paper houses conflagrations on the rise
mind and soul a purpose of ash
no red litmus test can pass
and gravity and poise and threatened
winds that pass like silk banners in a trance

to have to live with total recall
to revive the saddest or worst moments
in the brain's tarnished mirror day
after living day and look up to the skies
fractured in countless halves and prepared
to fall out of mind the destruction

of desires and passions the routine of
giving up this for that if only one could
have some of the loss back the faded
withered flowers garlands of the once bright
hues the face a loved one use to wear
is everything a deluded parade down
avenues dead-ended and shoulders that
barely sustain imponderable suffering
cathedrals of the knees hollowed out
buckled under the tumor of remembrances
each foot to go on why asks
the grass underneath the polar subjects
of multiply or divide the metal sheen
reflected back in ponds darkening with
fierce longing absence and cloud-work
the frame of a geography ill defined falling
asleep in the utter tangle of tenses
present or past the future is still hell

the fragments of myth and water never
subsiding in depths where ankles sink
bodies in tumult seizures and stains
aphasia in its harbor of stuttering vowels
shattered moonlight of memory
when regret and *pentimento* weigh
on a rumored conscience all too often
and daylight and the *missing*
person and the sun's haunted rays
who will gather the lingering dew
and make of it a wreathe ?

06-02-20

KYRIE ELEISON

world inflated by apocalyptic phonetics
about to explode with terrorist syntax
oblivious to the tented Olympian sky
menaced with extinction by the swollen
finger of the deity who governs nicotine
to which was led a rich pavilion colored
the flag of all hues and distances rioting
tear-gas and flash-bangs national physics
patrolling night starless incriminations
a judicial error in triplicate hives crystals
minutiae sprawling in the Cyclops' eye shot
blood hiatus mobilized in faux Greek O's
linger not *little ones* the death is here to
come nigh to the well and face down in
putty a smeared vowel an inherent
iota sub-script and tatter-eared dog
styled in late Romance vernacular high
each digit a fingered isolation in case
the point of verbatim and angelic hosts
a chord misfired from the orphic lyre
even as troubadours ricochet distances
of love seas and remote cliffs in despair
a trait at a time masked as a disease too
beautiful to endure oriental sheen each
with its coloration and page folio text
rewired and the way they sit there doe-
eyed the *Beatrices* and *Lauras* slowly
drinking chianti in the church vestry
clamoring for more complex statues
the talking kind and Sicilian puppets
that they are begin to mime and chant
contralto and soprano kyrie delusions
mystified by emergency room murals
pictographs idiolect in pre-Sumerian
sometime before the Flood and learn
for the first time to *die* given an envelope
full of hair-clippings from the day before
lonely solo saxophone in its very noon
when everything comes to a still point
but for locusts hidden in wheat sheaves
transparent wings flaring in swarms

bluish clusters in siesta formation
what the human shoulder suffers
lament-burdened in cycles of heat
that none can perceive yet mirror
sorrow in its leaf of unending echo

06-02-20

I AM ORESTES

not even the whole vowel half a vowel
uttered printed in air the rabid war cry
syllable after syllable in books turned around
the flames imbued in each consonant the uncounted
hatched and crossed out and the words
are they words ? mouthed in the wretched
styles of crumpled text and field the fanes
still smoking on the vivid backdrop the sound
of trumpet sistra drum-beat clamor and clangor
metal begets metal ! rivers of molten gold
eyes filled with the saturated airs of sky
blood-shot vernacular a hand a woven meter
wrists and fists and fingers plied with grasses
that talk and bleed and retreat and cry
have at me ! children bare-legged running
the morning dew-course and Aurora unfurling
her pinkish billows of memory the distances
of recall and atavistic ampersands and dry spells
weather that comes and goes through the Ear
of stone and lying down with archaic knee
the would-be hero dipped in the tallow
of premonition Fate and her eerie sisters the Furies
let the seas take us by the arms-full ! shouts
of glee the ankle strident with gore the depths
teeming with insect hap and shrike and gryphon
claim the heavens using only the number *Four !*
doubt is wonder and pyres ascend hills
of their own and outline the oblivion of Man
how is it torn and rent from the cloth ?
here and here the little shouts that pierce
the dark woof and stars at noon and spears
that riddle the hides of the sun spread out
like islands in the claustrophobic waters

let this be the reading ! let these be the statues
with their pages and pages of afternoon
and far beyond the resonance of mountains
where nymphs with hair of wasteland damp
forever with the impediments of speech
inventing with their seraphic voices *Death*
to entice the idiot human in the wandering wood
here take the staff and beat ! I am *ORESTES* !
it is ancient and it's not even tomorrow
the day that precedes the Day to come
linger in the weeds a softness of passion
delirium and the episode of the hip
flanked dyes vermilion and ocher that flare
in the western heavens a longing for *time* !
what ends before the following rhyme
and ever so the unfinished vowel
and dark the *hypnosis* of the gods

06-03-20

CIRCE DAUGHTER OF THE SUN

nostalgia for mud the thrice named One
sty and boudoir of voluptuous and transform
them into pig or bird wild-winged red-eyed
to supersede the self naming herbs and plants
for things no one dares touch or taste
me subsumed in catastrophe of vowels uttered
backwards into an Etruscan mirror where
misshapen heroes languor and longing their
armor tarnished tossed bent and rusted
the useless grammar of freedom captive
in skin and hide bristling in a trance of soil
wriggling roots fingers groping underground
in search of minds lost to rutting lechery and drink
a wine-vat a spent column of acanthus and ivy
and tomorrow the invention of machinery
oils and flasks of libation blood springs
and coils additives to make men see *again* !
hostess of light the wand all it gilds with its
painted aim asterisk and silver rim desire
like the moon spun out of control whatever
the sea spews forth maimed and catapulted

mortals always wanting more and bruiting crude
in slough and ditch let pattern of leaf overgrow
spreading malignant verdure in the overcast sky
cloud upon cloud define the afternoon a palace
where brassy templates small inscriptions
feminine and decay the paramount subject
of poetry recited by silent marble in long halls
of absence the final consonant to be avoided
hair braided in combs of blond bone from Egypt
magic ! incantation and oath curses strung
out like rosaries for all that can be holy
but *is* not and labyrinth of thought swirling sleep
penitential dreams fond caresses in depths
inky eyes that cannot look back and me
daughter of the sun bright folio of text
no abridgment simply the lengthy terrors
of narration and obscurity punctuation
of distance and mountains enormous with echo
alone abandoned to music of harp and flute
reciting back wordless declarations of love
night canceling the blown lamps of eternity

06-04-20

TROY

it was with some dismay that they could not
repair the machine that the ignition went cold
that dust and mist and obfuscation of memory
colluded to bring light to a close shut out the winds
could not see past the disarray of vowel and leaf
outside the glass and poorly attended the chapel
of prayers where the wheels with their bright flags
ceased turning no movement on the altar folded
with its curtains of names dredged from a past
of archaic stone and the mourning in the eaves
the flutter of distant wings sorrowing birds about
to take flight bearing with them vestiges of the soul
errant and sightless unable to count the days so
many unremembered that in the end are only
one sole day of life the tumult of incident and hap
the lists of accomplishments and failures what
of them ? scribbled in wax that exposed to the sun

will simply melt obscure mental jottings saying
I was here once ! the Latin class with its ancient
children bent over a puzzling map in pink and
green representing the shores of Troy and heights
in doubled browns and the waves lapping stone
and ships drawn up and recounted and singled out
which was the great hollow black one that would
carry them across to the Acheron one day ?

06-05-20

THE PHANTOM *HELEN*

did Helen round her vowels correctly
when the strange goddess came to visit
would she like other mortals mistake
the echoing sounds for the ringing in the ears
when the fatal arrow finds its mark
somewhere between kappa and rho ?
I too was born and schooled in arts
and the rule that purifies each sound we make
eternity released from cloudy occlusion
hid for centuries in obscure hills and
when mountains then reared their remote
peaks into unpronounceable heights
that was the age I too learned scansion
of archaic lines and beating time to meters
long forgotten and saying yes to the dreams
that promised languages both new and old
to render my mind a field of flowers and ponds
whence birds bathed in fresh light arose winging
effortlessly into a realm of song and ecstasy
pain and grief as well mingled in the goddess'
prophecies a sleep of dense rocky dialects
in her somnolent eyes turning deep blue
like shivering night descending to embrace
and hold tight phantom shapes with names
I had to memorize and stepping off a cliff
of rhyme plunge with despond into some
other world both above and below the place
where the sun blackens its fierce heat
and shines its massive beams on statuary
endowed for a moment with reason and sight

among them and speaking as if hypnotized
I felt the marble heart of time pulsating
impossibly in a syllable of stone and nacre
& seas tobacco-colored roiling against the wall
which petty kings had erected and hives
and the enormous leafy bower of myth
and the choice of breath or infinity
imbued the doubting spirit of ancient warriors
were I to cling to this thin sheen of reality
were I too to adhere to some foreign deity
a god who speaks French while sleeping a
diadem of curses and rolling dice and
hands excised of all property and the immense
imagined outer spaces galactic and rushing
without purpose ! all this encompassed
in my fevered brain the instant of awareness
at the same time the one of total loss
blindness of memory septic tanks covered
with mists of accident and hap the lure
of tomorrow as a *word* only as a word
and the rest of my life in search of Helen
a Helen become the ghost of all ghosts
pyramids in song only and sands mutilated
by the hours passing through waists of glass
some enigma some withheld mystery
never to be resolved however much
I learn by rote the echoing rules of
legendary vowels hidden in the leaf

06-06-20

THE RIDDLE

does the world end when the last consonant
can no longer be pronounced and whirlwind
efforts to restore speech to the statues that
though mutilated still maintain archaic dignity
and to give meaning to sounds uttered between
sleep and sleep and dreams exfoliate with echoes
leafy verbiage smoking accents rising dimly
into remnants of the heavens where acrostic
and phonetic decay strive for semantic reunion
the overwhelmed who people bedlam the mad

whose discourse is a bitten rope and memories
of taming horses with the Hittites 3000 BC
you are no more capable of rejuvenation
Allecto informs the Italic youth and mirrors
cracked in halves that cannot be and writing
becomes an issue between feuding deities far
above the daily melee and ears fill with maelstrom
and hands severed from the incantations that
condemned them stir in the uncanny realms
where shape and form no longer have content
ideas and aphasia the norms of temple ruins
stone piled on stone crevices where small grass
fingers its destiny and vowels escape like hissing
from the serpentine and longing assumes a depth
in lagoons where Nymphs perform solar rituals
making black the souls of those who transgress
almighty is the *Sun* ! he shakes his horses driving
his car through the crystalline spheres of eternity
careless as ever of the flames that devour and
ululating joylessly Naiad and water sprite embrace
bodies of mist and fog and revel in the art of dying
one syllable at a time the boundless lunar round
dividing everything they see into *night* and *time*
+ +
for why do you go to school to learn and what is
the focus of your vision and who lurking in bushes
are the rishis and bards whose mouths fill with
holy noises the reckoning of mortal illusions
judgment of the pyre and the comb ! disentangle
if you can the morass of rumor and thought
cannot piece together the conjunct hieroglyphs
carved on bone nor in what sense therein lies
the infinite riddle of light and breath

06-07-20

WHAT COMES AFTER OMEGA ?

for Fred and Joan-Marie Bauman

is the way toward knowledge Death ?
escape routes only lead to River Lethe
disposable bodies like shadows of ash
triremes lined up to dock at the Necropolis
holy the *indefinite* ! mountains take moon
and dissolve it in the *immemorable*
which is a reference to classical literature
statues become aphasic in the black dream
the sun is having as it orbits the unheard note
then Why ? the world survives in *italics* only
language remains an enigmatic cipher
in stone the ear yearns to resemble
itself in a cathedral of shoulders
and the inevitable grass wall blocks
echo and light from the architecture of time
the mourners who have wandered
astray from the hexameters of Virgil
are left to question the uses of sight
and the mechanics of smoke
is it for this there are *poets* without knowing why ?
trees simple as vowels and a headwind
that takes from earth its brightest children
stammer and stutter the Latin chords
ravel tongues and loosen the brain
with eerie tremors of a penultimate syllable
always surprised that the least of us
has been the first to find the *tumulus*
where the sun-letters lay buried
waiting to be unearthed in the next life
what !? there never was a beginning
only the strange ocher descent into day-light
wading into the Sargasso up to the knees
and then the Plunge the dark swell
that rises unawares to seize the rose
the centumfoliate *heart*
in the midst of the Gulf of Asia !
and what is more troubling than the thin
shivering rim out of which peer
the *souls* of the capsized the two thousand
and eight *Nameless* who remember us

though to us they are nothing but leaves
fragile countless trembling in the winds

06-08-20

NOSTALGIA

"*Oamenii sunt de patru feluri: cei care
nu s-au născut, cei care trăiesc, cei care
au murit şi cei care nu s-au născut, nici
nu trăiesc, nici nu au murit. Aceştia
sunt stelele.*"
   Mihai Cărtărescu, Nostalgia

*(There are four kinds of men: those who
have not been born, those who are alive,
those who have died, and those who have
 neither been born nor are living nor have
died. These are the stars.)*

what is more tenuous than breath the life force
even if air shatters into a thousand particles
do cling mortals to this thin invisibility
coerced by some blind desire to see beyond
the day's flapping portals and photographs
of the preterit existence the mind strives to
retain in dreams and do then step forth daylight
the surrounding maze of activity and silence
rounding out the vowels that sustain and then
taking in the colors fabricated by the eye roving
as it wakes from the dense surfeit and something
dismays the lessening glances in the lamp's
glare piled from on high the unseen horses gone
for a moment wild drag the solar cart to ruin a
devastating sound rocking earth's fixed pylons
does the avenue we stake as our daily claim really
exist as we measure paces or does the wavering
trance of wind and leaf betoken what cannot be
touched of this transitory realm we call *being* ?
shake from the sense of dread the calm and to
return to the book and verse and Juno's fierce ire
does then the hexameter break and a mountain
of distant hues dominated by red and the passion
felt but once it seems the very *love* that binds

souls atavistic and blind and do arrows begin
to smite the warrior class and meaning of echo
and reflection the mirror suspends in patterns
of the dream and come forth Angel it speaks
in fusion of consonant and beam the arched
heights we seek to enter the leveled sands and
weights of planetary delusion aspire we to move
as shuttles on a loom forsaking reason left to
chance the errant aim mistaking masks for men
shadow wights spackled dots on a shifting landscape
waterfall and remote mists and the rush of a
single summer through the sleeping ear of stone
endless imbued the vast array as dark unfolds
the interior of the unspoken word enormous
peopled by memory of the unborn in us who
trek through temple ruins to be as stars

06-09-20

THE WEIGHT OF MEMORY

how much does memory weigh ?
a feather a grain of sand the thin line
that crosses the hand's palm of fate
a single hair or the force of the indefinite
article employed by the Masters of Death
the shadow of night and the child who was
skipping the sidewalks just a minute ago
now gone from the field of gravity a snip
of a color torn from the last shirt he wore
does memory weigh as much as the first tear
grief and sorrow assumed in a separate vowel
or is it the fierce trajectory of the Sanskrit arrow
the fulminating crescent in an absent heaven
that appears just once in a lifetime
only to be forgotten the following day
that it ever was that sleep can be measured
by the metric system that a finger maybe two
are the equivalent of lawns darkening
on the hill-slope that informs a hospital bed
a ward of the state a mind that has no halves
a thought simply escaping like air from a valve
in the great and rusted machinery of breath

or perhaps the load of punctuation asterisks
and ampersands dissolving in clouds
or ink no heavier than the myth it draws from
water turned to steam and mist fogs pushing
slowly through the mountain on the west-side of time
chemical signatures for unseen elements
spirits the *soul* itself un unexplained etymology
the wavering consonants of decomposition
gods of incense and fragrance who have no body
memory the echo buried in stone the day after
the birth of space and all of earth rounding
its powerful atmosphere of failed quadrants
of a geometry of chalk and dust red powders
affiliations of words to things that lack substance
syllables like the zzing and zzzoom of bees
that haunt the ear with minute skies of distance
or is memory simply the nothingness
the verbatim zero of a wind-inscription
blowing through the injustice of destiny
the ineffable and imponderable rattling
of accents and tones and fault-lines
black as antimony on the scales of an after-life
or is it only the briefest sensation of
heat circling the frieze of a lost summer
the voice interred in the leaf or
the trembling fever of infinity ?
no weight like memory that burdens
the human cathedral with its shoulders
that sink and totter with the shift of years
error of person skin and mask
more than that memory freighted is with
eternal regret for that irretrievable
moment missed the *last*

06-10-20

TEOCALLI

for Joe who appeared yesterday morning
for a fraction of an instant in the doorway
standing in the light of the morning sun
confused with radiance and dazzling
the stanzas of an unwritten poem shift
in the monumental distances of air
crane-feathered shafts rotate like minds
ablaze in the pyramidal distances of sky
stone built on stone stepping to heaven
solar flares like tongues speaking loud
the destructions of cloud and thunder
and ever deeper the effects of amnesia
rain drowning cities of fine dust citadels
of bone and tumult havoc of wheels
spun out of control bringing down all
ten directions and mountains reared
overnight to mark off the western margin
where the archaic sea darkens rushing
to mirror itself in a dream of feathers
and the *twins* up and down they go
tracing each periphery of rock and grass
measuring how far it is to the lunar aleph
fading like dissolved aspirin at dawn
what fills the ear at such an early hour
if not the Sanskrit parrot reciting
chronologies and adamantine dynasties
names none can rightly recall inscribed
on the reverse of coins or obliterated
by a mere thumb on porous sandstone
libraries ! the tomb of words and to speak
the labyrinthine dialects communing
with deities of the Unseen and Unheard
pages torn at random from the codex
depicting the origins of divine Chaos
night ! splendors of ink in canyons
where the dead revive use of their hands
such a morning atop the *great* Teocalli
converting sums of air into breathless voice
hail all the heights and renown of fire !
we have come down the Panamerican
visiting *each* of the summers of 1953

and talking backwards to mummified
relatives wrapped in serapes of liquid gold
we will never reach tomorrow for sure
the Nymph *death* will take one of us
before the prophesy can be fulfilled
every day is this single bright moment
standing like phantom pharaohs immobile
in the pellucid movie film of memory
you are me and I am you ! there is grass
and maps strewn all over the lawn
and avenues that stretch as far back as
the first city carved out of the womb
ten minutes apart the matching Teocallis
that cast no shadow only black light !

06-11-20

THE GARDEN OF PROSERPINA

the great islands of Silence that float effortlessly
though *mind* leaving no trace and the Spain
of lost sunsets of burials of mountains
of donkeys tethered to echoes of mourning
the last of all rocks and stone and waters
darker than the eaves of Pluto's mansion
whatever requires no punctuation of thought
all of space reduced to its thimble of light
and sleeping forever in the marble estuary
of childhood the enormous flowers of memory
drained of color darkening even more as
the stellar ascension draws nigh and the horses
of Dawn the magnificent ruddy and black
steeds striking their iron hooves on the anvil
whence both Aetna and Vesuvius arise moaning
bereft of their dreams of fireflies and bees
hives that have never been ! quarrels with
insect kingdoms with lunar realms of ink
dusky unending evenings of planet Saturn
forgetting everything about geometry and
leaning hard into the curvature of Chaos
Proserpina comes up for air ! *Primavera !*
to the right and left peninsulas and cliffs
Chinese waterfalls and mists of longing

to have the *mind* back and to *see* with total
recall talking in the original Ionian dialect
sitting down backwards in an Etruscan glass
writing and writing everything there is
about hair and combs and perfumes and
bangles fifty on each arm and bright anklets
made of Dravidian gemstones and henna
maps of the *Cosmos* in red on the soles
of her feet and patterns of vowels and drums
triangles and radios that go on and off singing
pyramidal madrigals using only leaves and buds
phonic elements of the atmospheres swirling
in gusset and hem-stitching and epic cloudbursts
all summer long and nowhere to go that *grief*
won't accompany her gathering as she meanders
through fields of poppies and liquid emeralds
the words for *breath* and *light* with fingers
like harp-strings striking unheard notes
in the hour's unraveling twilight
and what else ! furrows plied by gold fish
intent on returning to *Cocytus* with tassels
and embroideries of syllabic ruins pronouncing
the revival of night that vast underground
spackled with eternities of illusory stars
and in an instant *she* disappears again
into *mind's* haunted and empty labyrinth

06-11-20

FOOTNOTE TO ILIAD IV, 52

the broad streets of Mycenae

I just heard Mary Lou's voice in the late sun
of my life even as god quarrels with god
high flown words epithets and destruction
of cities each in their own design a word
adolescent in the fane sacred to Demeter
fields as they open and hell underneath
have so many years rushed like falling cliffs
upon my head you ask their eyes flashing
demons not goddesses wristlets and head-bands
the war camps murmuring like hives of unrest
will plunge spears through her vowels and

yet cooing as a mourning dove and fling
carelessly of the halls filling between classes
with kids inglorious of mien and hurtling
oaths to never yield and demanding back
for ransom captured slave girls pinafore
and frock penny-loafer for the dance the
great ballet of death they call it in Minoan
age rock carvings fragments of speech huge
with unpronounceable consonants the statues
we used to be stammering on the court-house
lawn with the civil war cannon rusting and Priam
in his motel weeping over his hundred in a harem
already dark with unending twilight corpses
of birds omens and satellites filled with blood
racing through the cloud-work is there more
to tell of the fray at mid-afternoon greaves
and splinters a golden rod a branch with which
to enter the Underworld drugged with perfumes
exotic notions to translate by tomorrow the
opening lines the walls erected on the west side
cicadas golden insects bees and humming birds
to be worn in the hair and sing as befits a
Job's Daughter ear to the text of silence echo
pursuing syllables and come to a stop the horses
to drink of the river and watching in their eyes
the first stars of night rise baleful with glimmers
the wasted otherness in exclamation marks a
height of drowsy splendors if only one could
catch the night-train home the bed where
I am to lie in state the deathless enmity of
the deities in a halting early Attic Greek
filling the ear with nonsense and noise cryptic
as the unfolding of time
me here eighty-one and a half years old
and so many gone in reverie and stupor
how many books left to read ?

06-12-20

LITTLE DEUCE COUPE

life such as it is
you had to take that hairpin curve
the guys back at the filling station warned you
now it's just a contemplation
like that rainy night in Green Gulch
who could predict the future ?
poetry readings and horse-back riding
small trophies in aluminum and mercury
so why was sunset denied to us ?
sitting almost in a trance in some eatery
ignored by the bonzes in their orange-fade
which year was it ?
the hour that has no sister
and the length of the winding roadway
all the way to southland where the dead
the ones who didn't look back
in the rear-view mirror to see what was coming
the enormous lack of sky at that moment
like an unexpected infection in the mouth
you didn't know and let go of the wheel
dining was never the same again
at Nepenthe looking down at the ocean
all rock and banging surf
what was the accompanying music like ?
green always green scum- or sea-green
the lyrics were inaudible something about
a *little deuce coupe* whatever that is
it was California a place to die
master plans about zen and not-understanding
arms akimbo eyelids fluttering
the great apogee when nothing manifests
in a matter of minutes the epiphany vanished
whirlwind tour of the missing continent
mountain reduced to its primordial inch
buried in snow in the High Sierra
the mistaken resort hotel
vacancies in neon and false advertising
where to stop and eat next ?
now it's actually today bathed in ink
when no words hold EVERYTHING running fluid
the mind and its vast abscess

told you not to take that hairpin curve
little deuce coupe

06-13-20

VENUS IN THE PANDEMIC

". . .et dictis divinum adspirat amorem"
Aeneid, VIII, 373

code calls for calm across the many seas
battered and broken the boats sails ripped
from masts and hands upheld in appeal
to the divine forces who imbue the soul
with glimmers brighter than salt-crystal
mid afternoon sun-swell agonies and grief
misspelled on banners torn in the wind
will nothing chasten the world's torment
devoid of presence the elements rush
in a turbo-jet of frenzy and nymphs arrayed
on beaches of black sand keep singing
through meshes of radiography and alchemy
humans upended in their reading of history
jade and basalt ledges where they teeter
weeping hard into the leaf and calling out
names only half remembered as the list
increases in length and breadth of vowel
and tonic accent and notions of tea-time
and hours spent translating the abacus
of obituaries in rooms quickened with sorrow
do you know them ? quizzes on electricity
and drumheads and porphyry and shells
blown into the eastern quarter of sky as
if to summon from the ossuary horses
slain in enigmatic wars around the bend
I have nothing to show for it faded voice
cries out from its newspaper wrapping
earth is convulsed whether to re-enter
the ice-age or throw chance to the abyss
mountains and jungles of liana grass burn
exclamation marks and proportion of smoke
spirit world nothing more than a graph
showing the spike in kovid-19 fatalities
it will never be tomorrow again ! suffer *all*

the map is withdrawn the texts deleted
fingers scrawl the words for grass and time
on a lunar slate fallen from the heaven
of asphalt and envy listening for the small
echo of sleep interred in the marble ear
where it whispers the eternal child is gone
forever from the counterpoint of memory
+ +
if only Venus would prosper again in
her perjured skin and kimono of red gesso
her thought a labyrinth of desire and heat
recalling heroes whom she bore blazing
through generations of epic hexameter
her mind the hazard of a temple ruin
in her fleeting glance the turbulence of light
yet does she with glyphs of rumor instill
divine love into the mortal ruin
a dazzle despite the day's futile end
as she steps deftly among the fireflies
and asterisks aglow in deathless night

06-14-20

FEAR OF FALLING

it is finished cold through the limbs
courses a cloth of light wound around
the temples though ruin is in advance
the field ahead a mere strip of conscience
weathers of ancient snows and dim the
memory of the hill and trees bared by
winds so-called inevitable can no longer
hold discourse by the table where sit
phantoms nodding off their vacant heads
plied by dementia or madness the thinking
is to void the written stones the litmus
ruddy or azure with its pronouns and
second to none the riverbanks washing
away can a finger no more point than
the fragile bone the fear of falling a portent
from on high as they say unwelcome as
scavenger birds come to pluck at eyes
that see nothing razed to the ground a

form of movement did not hear in the night
and crashed like a rotted trunk branches
devoid of leaf and the talking whistling
in the ears can it be dreaming is it best
to sleep and wake no more wan the lamps
flicker the smallest lashes and glassy out
there wavering and for once not mention
yesterday afternoons in the gelid sun laid
bare on the hide spread to dry of oblivion

06-15-20

IPHIGENIA

fierce forth go to the seas seething
with ships caulked black at the prow
and to speak of Iphigenia and Achilles
arrows spent in the thrust of ropes
sails the shattered linens tied to masts
a pointed finger from the ire of deities
bind and spell to the death mortal envy
greed to plunder and ransack Asia
cities in toil furled in dusky banners lion
and leopard the strangers in midst
of cloud bane and fustian glamour to sing !
archaic rock portions and vowels left to
drift in the marine anger of the first hour
roseate slumbered the horses dappled
shaking off the onus of direction and
wild as in dreams hurtle through crescent
flame snorting Greek sophistry a hand at
a time each carefully placed on a quoit
of sound the advance of language tutelary
divinities scattered by the white munitions
of philosophy and what is more total
the Furies in ambush hard by the streets
of Mycenae in eventide of shadow and
plots of homicide beautiful oceans of
memory set asunder will they ever reach
the midpoint let alone the ends of time
whichever has an arm the baleful spear to
thrust wounds made in a simple of grass
and fuses to blow the asterisms out of

their punctuation planets rolling ablaze
in the mountains of chaos a splendor
to recite the dead who are forced to forget
abandoning person and soul to the flowers
brightly risen on the new turf of verse
elongated consonants and awnings of night
descending in waves of foaming sleep
the untimed clock registered in the heart
in which dialect will it explode the fumes
a device of echo and beyond so raise
the sacrificial knife and count back
to the moment when oblivion began

06-16-20

PARVATI

bees and jewels and honey-colored hair
lotus stalks and elephant trunks and loud
the crowns that fit the waning moon
her eye is sundered by a thousand rays
like suns that never finish rising
grasses that twine and weeds that shout
heaven's pearl melts into a milky sea
if her feet lift a metropolis is revealed
of emerald and everlasting basalt below
great sand-hills that forge skies for ants
and bone-yards and fossil graves of water
shining like the final asterisk of time
the distance it takes for mountains to
be born and how she climbs and where
she comes to rest on seats of ivory tusk
legends of combs and parted braids and
longing for the home she never had a
relief in stone with parts of words none
can ever read and tempests that swirl
inside the color red and winds of palms
farther south than the landfall of the dead
how swift she shakes the whisk-broom
emptying it of time and the precious
vacancies of space that hang like tassels
from her brow and why is it we never
see the sections of her immensities a body

the hue of over-ripe tamarind or amber
vague whorls left by escaping planets
and the echo of brass or copper in the air
five thousand bracelets jangling on her arms
and ear-rings the size of ink or porphyry
and lip-gloss in tons and wagons that
bear her shadow from tomb to tomb
pulled by oxen gravid with unreal destinies
garlands of skulls two-hundred by the inch
heaps of steaming entrails and spoons
the shape of the islands of the sun
how vast the depths perceived in her glance
labyrinthine tracts of thought a mind
formed by a memory of thunder that
destroys the million hemispheres of the brain
where countless the *shivas* and *buddhas*
meditate on infinity in a single blade of grass
poetry ! dew-drops skeletons of electricity
fish that ply the underside of tiny leaves
that spring from the empty vowel left behind
in her voice's ecstatic redundancies

06-17-20

canción del parque Chapultepec

cronología del aire ! arquitectura de las nubes !
soy de poco valor
que lástima ! las abejas en sus columnas verticales
de azul incendiado chupando chupando los huesos
de la hierba dormida
soy azteca
soy caldeo
soy de mucho valor
sierras de sueño blanco que veo nomás
cuando estoy nadando en mi césped de memorias
todo verde desde el hombro izquierdo de césar vallejo
hasta la rodilla derecha de garcía lorca
acumulando los dos las muchas muertes de la luz
aunque vivimos como momias en Tenochtitlan
apenas sufriendo el tránsito de los motores de las plumas
yo lo único que soy es la luna
chafada y transparente como aspirina a mediodía

y hay mares invisibles que suben los pirámides de la frontera
pistolas con ojos !
ahí viene la bala !
dame mi caballo corrompido
yo soy peruano
el úlitmo dios soy
el mero dios de la basura hieroglífica de chapultepec
fumando como nunca las chispas baratas
de las olas que han venido a ahogar el estado de california
poco a poco y a menudo con sus pronombres
y hierro de lenguas mas muertas que el sol negro
tapadera y tumba del fuego silencioso
de mis pasos en el jardín unitario de la duda
y por eso digo
yo soy

06-17-20

LOST IN TRANSLATION

whiz zing missiles sharpened projectiles
darkening the air sun-blot and cloud press
how many the thousands chariots elephants
horses and warrior-heads scattered on earth
glittering like blood-bathed jewelry the whole
a cry from the heart a verse torn out of the ear
entering the world of total silence a version
of this appears later in chronologies and
obituaries and started but not finished epos
or imperfect newspaper accounts of how this
and that war began and which god said what
to another god rambling parenthetical remarks
a day in the life of an anonymous et cetera and
the ringing in the brain and fossils of water and
the enormous variety of air and winds tempests
swirling and churning the multiple dictionaries
of sea and sand the regatta fitted out with gold
and silver and sheets of crimson silk flapping
in the gorgeous sleep of the appointed admiral
who can remember all the details drowning
and elaboration for a life between the pages
woke up one morning with a name fixed in mind
and set forth and patted the dog on the way out

mowed the lawn raked the leaves peddled the bike
delivered the papers envied the porches of the rich
went to school and grew up so to speak
a statue with a panoply of words and subjects
to write or be written off the beautiful canopy
casting shade the heat of the afternoon a day
at a time until the cumulation dazzles sun-spent
overtures to women in the key of delta and trance-
dancing in the marriage boat and children to come
or to die unawares and tragedy and grief why
it all happens what is the cause and root and sky
dizzy overhead indifferent yes indifferent
whiz the zing the fling and flung spears and horses
rutting beasts chariots spun out of control all
in a day in the life of and still what does the vowel
and what is its quantity and occlusives and stops
dire discord carved in iron and Anubis barking
speech transfer and ultimately all-pervasive
SILENCIO

06-18-20

THE DEPTHS

OK what's next ?
      countdown to infinity
am I only an echo ?
despond and the greater but unfinished
epics the *tristitia* and the origins and
whatever else involves the *heroic* heart of man
is that a question revolving its nexus
or merely the abstract reflection of the
sun rising blackened out of its orient
bathed in the liquors of light and absence
and to shed the lamp-luster on this day
negritude and dissolution the endless
bottoms of the inky sea of mind !
where have I been all my life ?
tremendous events have already occurred
father's day in the antipodes
gift-giving among the dead who struggle
to relive the instant of their going out
am I the ancient thing timing this accident ?

radios and spark plugs and main-streets
illuminated by holiday parades in the multiple
hues of red and coronations of homecoming queens
paper dolls cutout from magazine covers
ready to burn and soap-operas
of nefarious ball-room love-affairs
menacing antidote to the ennui of fiction
write the poem and over with it !
verses of Cybele hoyden of the archaic
rock-face as she rushes headlong into disaster
the echelons of sleep strung out pointlessly
even as the car misses the turn and goes hurtling
such are the minimal fusions of memory
I am at once either no more
or continually reliving an insignificant moment
from my unremembered childhood
the *Depths* ! futility of words to organize !
it will be a hymn of longing in the grasses
wet with the dews of eternity
I am gone as are we all
into the tenebrous arcana fluttering
shadow of an unseen leaf

06-19-20

AFTER SCHOOL

it's as if Europe had never existed
nor the cries of the gods in their birth pangs
only the rains solemn but inconstant
in their livery haunting oceanic memory
was it alone or twice dead the specter
presumed at sleep's eternal doorway
lintel of shadow-sky and essence of grief
the fortuitous numbers exposed to the tempest
the ships and barks and rafts and timbers
tossed upside down in the brief squall
of printer's ink and a lifetime relived
unwanted in the umbratile passage to the
here and back and fossil reverie in fade
the suggested memento in a shop window
deathless girlfriends lingering at the counter
to try a spray of bad perfume mispronouncing

the French etiquette attached to the label
a promise to come back to life as a cloud
infrequent as the cream about the dancer
dressed in marble and what else can one
expect waiting for the opposite shore
to arrive with its big Asian head-dress
a worn encyclopedia volume and rent linen
shreds of satin and canvas flapping distraught
I know who that used to be exclaims a voice
disembodied and faintly august in the late
imagined lamp flooded with fireflies
again and again we open the yearbook
but the photos are no longer intact
no finger exists that can point to the one
who should have been there at the podium
reciting as ever the endings of poetry
lilac-fragrance distance and longing

06-20-20

ODE : FATHER'S DAY 2020

mountain shadows and burning peaks
lives but shadows in the restless embers
remember the day before when jumping
from a pram you collided with angels
a thousand of them strong in their wistful
blue satins winging deathlessly toward the west
a long time it was writing that sublime accident
a troupe of circus-swells with painted cardboard faces
and shouting from the bleachers it was midnight
it was life as printed in the book of Lies and
you in the mangle of wings and tufts and spears
imagined elephants and riders blackened by the sun
midnight spores of breath and buds of lotus red and
azure stalks tender as the children you have lost
and hands like grasses pulled from fossil earth
and the massive vowels moving in the winds to spell
a year or two you think to live the survival of the few
a situation followed by its consequence of hues
and shades and oriental embroideries how is it kings
have names and employ slaves to carry their consonants
yet you down here in the fallen tents and ropes still

strive to prop the verse of the summer tempest
with syllables borrowed from archaic stone
fragments of words illusory temple shards and seas
heaving their surging breasts against the cliffs
of destiny or so they say rampant lions and leopards
and heroes who've forgotten how to sing looking
for a way back from hell having no fixity of mind
enormous hospital of illusion sick-bays and fevers
that leave their beds astray and crumpled license
like sheets to wave in the battered southern storms
the dead as many as they are keep reclaiming
their share of mortal sleep but statues such as
we are jealousy and rage and fomented inks
how can we speak to them ? the world lies on the
other side of time the life we designed around
a single love the treasured irretrievable
this day of all the most is depth and sorrow
utterly intransigent we weep in storehouses of memory
and climb from rock to rock in this dream
both bedlam and hive of maddened bees a hem
and a stitch undone the brain as it tries to speak
I knew him when he was a brother
I knew him when he was a son

06-21-20

SOME VIRGILIAN STROPHES

it was out for the sun one day a wrinkle and dot
spotted over the eye and what a bright
the fantastic rush of blooms to greet the lamp
that exercises horse and atmosphere in a single
glorious moment and heights too of ineffable
and the whole section erased from history
verses of books tied by a slender thread
of energy swifter than epistles to and from
Mars the exegetical brief about salvation
followed by torrents that drown the beleaguered
fleets seeking entry into illusion's map

what a tour of darkness the sleeper undergoes
no meadows here no pastoral glances with a flute
no meadows down and hapless brooks that run
like silver wires through a poet's mind

how far away childhood the remembered golden
vessel the branch and leaf of symbology and
at the same time enclosed in the flying spear's
intent divine retribution for the gift of light
quickened highway speed that grief only brings

is longing now the disease of man the distance
it takes a line of words that exhaust all sense
vowels flung into the void and voices ghostly
from the recording of the Orphic death and high
as remote notes the singing in the mountain
alas I die the mummer's cry and shapeless clouds
that fill the eye and hard by the running shore
the beached and broken boats and corpses standing
still the ready call to disembark and fight !

so much did I love my friend and now shadows
toll the archaic refrain with carved sounds of brass
that tremble the afternoon's long denial and
six by twenty the gods who frown gazing down
at hill mounds and clusters like ants engaging
cities for a round of sleep the dense and darkened
moment when the catafalque is prepared and
memory of all renown is laid to perpetual rest
alas he was the One a voice of sopranos garlands
the fading air with paper flowers and dusky ink
the unsighted planet careens ablaze in dreams
that none can decipher and place the stone
deep within the head's uncovered consonant
the last and silent echo of the unburdened leaf

each is the time to wound and still the syllables
of oracle and island and watch as seas lay down
their arms and rock and cavern fill with evening's
small bestiary the lightless world we now must go
and as shadows moving signs and sorrow a memory
can no more define the living it was on the edge
a blade of grass and eighty-one enigmatic years

06-22-20

MIASMA

so we prayed to Apollo like they told us
at daybreak and by noon the rutilating motions
of the stars visible was cause for tremors
earth a little tipsy trying to stabilize
and offered up mantras and small sacrifices
and built a big altar like a garden of wild
fragrances and bees in clusters like continents
and the whole air an activity of consciousness
summoned the names of mythical bards
angry with what little results and besought
the god and fretted over the lyre strings
and at once arose great dust storms
swarming from Ethiopia mushrooming silently
over the European fragment and justified
by none of our pretenses went out to the oil-fields
to see how quickly they might burn a holocaust
of the atmospheres reckless dividends of the suns
as they duplicated each blacker than the other
each assuming its own propitious hour and
driving in our remodeled vehicles upcountry
charging the various temples and fanes
a ruin of worshipping the tattle-tale rumors
about Helen and the dog-faced courtesans
of Troy in their wilting curtains of pansy and lotus
a blossoming of hillsides and the road that
dead-ended by the quagmire how else could we ?
the moment had come and gone !
the god's twin sister with her argent bow and
violent quivers sent into the empyrean to bring
down planets and constellations the shape of stag
or deer and fleet of foot in her haunted woods
would a fix by the Stygian bank be suitable ?
puzzled by the hiatus looming ahead the heavens
a large gaping cicatrix or a wound running with ichor
streams of the gods dazzled by their own self-deceit
reckless with epithets and oaths and the circular
paths that destroy unity and the world as wide
as it seems a mere punctuation in the passing void
assembled with our hosts armored and jeweled
it was only a countdown before night's spawned
confusion of asterism and astrological conjecture

would bring us into its unsettling infinity
embracing us in our own futile hap and gore
mysteriously aligned with the oracles that maze
of corruption greed and royal adultery multiplied
by the names of Cassandra and Clytemnestra
the endings with their pitiable cries and moans
like birds sent into the Mountain of sleep
and what else ? Apollo god of distance and Light
sounding his jazz that echoes through rock
and the chaos of memory

06-23-20

PHILOSOPHY 2020

the fault lies at the back of things
desolation and silence of rock fragment
at high noon haunted by spirits of the tragic line
lunatic stitching of invisible hands approaching
the limit and beyond that hiatus and abyss
dizziness of the thwarted asterisk blackening
on its daily tour of the heavens blinded and
eroded by the embers of despair flinging wing
and trestle overboard into the seething seas
sounds of hissing and viviparous steam
rising to envelope the terms for uncertainty
and fear among pronouns of the 2nd person
lost in honorific delusion of consonant clusters
diphthongs and aborted syllables like statues
headless & maimed on the avenue that leads
to the quarry of birth and death
is it syntax and warning ? what is the decibel
that reaches planet mercury first ?
the old gods in their worn sandals drinking ouzo
wander careless and mocked in shop windows
waiting for the photographer to shed his hood
alive no more ! events that occur on a spear-tip
legends of heroes running amok in steep ravines
or nymphs thirty in all wasting by the dry well
of Castalia and what else is new in this century
of speculation and myth the lapping census
of waves come to naught in Ionia
day-long blanks & vocal presences of the *unseen*

while one by one the numbers up to twelve
sequenced in an order of infinity and madness
like stoics and epicureans lapsed in their cups
who argue illusion and tautology of the Negative
redundancies of propositional logic
deities with their counterfeit breath
endowing mortals with great promises of language
as if to construct immortality in the apse of reason
despite the errant circularity of heat and
spheres of reckoning and doubt the universe itself
the dwindling exclamation mark of distance
is to go home an option anymore ?
memory when only twenty four hours remain
what is it good for ?
the hospital bed and the tinker's cart
each in their own way an entrance to Hades
riverrun fast the five streams unwinding
beneath the apologetics of *mind*
fire and ice the labyrinth of elements
hydrangeas and hollyhocks drowsing in the driveway
waiting for the evolution of the vowel
and the famous sleep of bees within
the sun's enormous and empty tomb

06-24-20

THE ELUSIVE MOMENT

is ninety-nine only a question mark
set by the fates to endure half a second more
what follows in the ruin of memories
but the chasm and abyss of solitude
amid rock fragment and echoing murmur
sleeping in the ear of distance lament
and grief the irretrievable sum of accidents
breath and light and the winsome leaf
stirring in the wind's cavernous voice
tenuous architecture of dreams vanishing
inside the haunted vowels of the oracle
will we be visited by gods after all ?
between the temples an oceanic roaring
gigantic whisper of the archaic extends
an invisible hand to explore the remnants of air

the encyclopedic formation of the clouds
the furious and single attribute of a storm
purpling the hem lines of a hieroglyphic page
grammar of the constellations syntax of night
everything collapses in the thimble of fire
held to the unseeing eye and verging on
nothingness the mind struggles to accept
the enigmatic consonants of a prophesy
never sure whether the divine is that
thing within that stirs *sound* into meaning
when all afternoons circulate in the heat
that defines the instant of self-awareness
only to lapse back into the dusky mountain
at the far west of time and the fading
margins of cognition and absence

06-25-20

FOOTNOTE TO THE MAHABHARATA

heard it all the nonsense the ruses idioms dialects
distortions of sound plangent echoes synonyms of grief
for the sorrowing who live in southland of the dead
shadow and hieroglyph cloud and thunder blotted
lamps blackened sun said it all out loud or dreaming
in stone or wafer thin blood-lines in atmospheres run
afoul of the gods whose counterfeit breaths and faked
dalliances sounded the drum shook the sistra blew
the mighty sea-conch felled trees on invisible mountains
generated lie after lie about the human condition would
not relent even in poetry to mitigate the tempest hush
the seas in their night-dramas evolving vowel and
pitch and the distances too eloquence and diaphragm
of punctuation stellar miasma and tragic declamation
high-school yearbooks burnt in the vicinity of the ear
libraries and mausoleums each interred in the small
inch of soil on the other side of noon remembered only
partially the ways of the hour the discourse of nymph
and reason the debate between soul and corpse always
the heights to contend and the plazas and vacant lots
automobile graveyards and shipwrecks not the least
the children spooling their kites long afternoons in
the imitation of Elysium prams and strollers and bikes

rusting in forty day rains and signs of the afterlife and
clepsydras and Egyptian fortune-tellers and *vedic* thoughts
about the triangle revolutions in mind and dialysis and
trumpet-vines and the whole verbiage about salvation
minutes spent in the organ-grinder's circle ambition and
rebirth the numismatic intent of history the fierce and
forced clerks who govern the state and penchants for war
and spear and diastole and chips inserted in the brain will
we ever and what else is new centuries after fate has run its
course distilling language on pedestals of broken bone and
trumpeting a hollow victory elephants running amok
in the carnage of the Mahabharata reduced to a list of
the names of ten thousand and eleven maharajas and
who will ever say that memory has a role in this lengthy
rigamarole alphanumeric passions to overcome heat and
the woman who used a perfume called opium and hotels
where finally the encumbered of heart come to die

06-26-20

ALL OF US

"rex Iuppiter omnibus idem"
Aeneid, X, 112

they call it *avidya* when the shadowy sisters sing
and all about darkness covers the fronds and
who can tell which is the way out of the mind
and which forever is the memory of light
we have come this far and no farther a grammar
and a lexicon and grassy knolls underfoot and
the presage of a day when together we shall knit
the sun's passage as a unit of gravity a great
and burning instant when pronouns will be
discarded and one by one we will intuit heaven
the very distance in time when birth no longer matters
a section of rock will fall heavily into the waters
like the echoes of a fragment of death faint
with prehistoric vowels and a floating cluster
of consonants to convey what once was weightless
you and I in the dance of grass and dew the loss
of all contour the shape and density of air
embraced yet sundered in opposite directions
an eye and an ear fourfold or geminated the whole

revolving around cognition and meaning and
waking back to the first hour when semblances
of mountains marked for flight wavered distantly
I am alive! from somewhere a voice from sheets
of ocean pinkish shells and corolla tenderly wrapping
the brain into evolutions of flame and ivy
that nothing will come of nothing and born and
walking and taught to fly and wingless to fall
to earth once and for all the child of misnomer
and intellect fable of letters unwritten and
fused to the inks of myth and led to move in
mysteries saying nothing that can be repeated
and enormous with *otherness* the vacuum of being

so this is what it is unable to discern between
what has happened and what has only been dreamed

all of us

06-26-20

PIRATE AND TRAVELER

to break with the earth but a remnant of memory
prows and rock heights discerned the sleep of
immortals gilded profound drugged with illusion
to create and floral abysses and the width of inks
spilled across the blank page and of time and its
corollaries and the spuming audacious seas of
outer space that occupy the inch of mind aflame
with discourse of the forgotten the childishness
inherent to ambition like as not to drown in folly
the increment of light spreading slowly before it
evaporates and the lawn where we spent our
first eternity watching the sky's performance
using geminated consonants as actors in the parade
soon as summer's over ! yes and double the joined
ends the multiple sections of the left eye as it regards
the ladders and suits the preamble to all that is
destined to disappear forever you know what I
mean this automatic flow of syllables incantations
of the void and vowel and excess orientation of love
who as the epistle unwinds word over word and
spear and cloud and thunderbolt the panoply of

epic recitation strutting the incunabula of thought
come on ! you know it's all over there's no more
ignition in the process the shadows have vacated
their bodies in full accent and tone and bluish highs
inhaling that intense smoke waiting for the unheard
jazz drumming in the ear where the entire month of
July semaphores its aching recall of heat and Lo !
the bereaved and their costumes of tears and opera
how can I not sing more this ? chances of a second
life a different way of embroidering the speech act
the temple of magnificent Ruin the embolism working
its way to the communication center and Kaboom !'
effortless dusts adorn whatever remains of the plot
you and me ! wearing the same shirt squabbling
over the map where it says in hieroglyphic *red*
that this afternoon will never come to pass and like
the man in front of the burning bush all fades
the distinct and the variable the immense and
futility sitting there on the curbstone waiting just
waiting for the Friend who is the mask of death
to manifest with his game of pirate and traveler
Remember ?

06-27-20

DARK AS IT EVER WAS

> *"Stat sua cuique dies, breve et inreparabile tempus*
> *omnibus est vitae"*
>   *Aeneid, X, 467-468*

to each his appointed day brief and irreparable
the time to live ceded to all and so forth
each numbing dawn as it begins a wheel invisible
yet ablaze the mind slowly and what the eye captures
in the distances of nostalgia a mountain
no higher than ink and even farther west
the lonesome decibels on the compass used
for stellar navigation in a post mortem world
dedications to the seraphim who have silenced
the song with their evanescent vowels and the power
of misgiving and doubt the grief of the instant
when earth turns itself over to look deep within
asking what was it all for the love intruding the body

clothed in the despair and rage of false assumptions
life everlasting the heavens in tripartite dissolution
triumphant aspects of recurring dreams about
and all the rest of the paraphernalia of contemplation
a Buddha here a Buddha there of stone or haze
the matrix of evolution dominated by fish wild and
unconscious becoming ever gradually the thing that
walks on its hind feet and thinks to *soar*
the damned have never left us the dearly departed
have become invisible the jazz of kaleidoscopic thought
if only we could keep it riffing and yet we cannot
the door opens part way to the abyss footsteps
crushing the pansy bed outside the dormer window
I am never to have it back ! sufi indistinction of being
and memory on the top rung of its ladder
where smoke and sleep have empire and far below
the world with its animated cartoons of ants and bees
and rock fragments that stand out in raging waves
the child it must have been to suffer such a blow
and the various stages of coma and aphasia
and the debilitating side effects of reason
when it comes to counting backwards who can
control the steering wheel ?
the struggle to remember even the shape of
a single leaf shaking in the oncoming night
dark as it ever was the loss

06-28-20

ποίησις

nor do the cars cease moving up and down
of the gods in pursuit of their immortality
nor woods on mountain slopes and torrents
speeding through rocky crevices and vales
to seas surging wrathfully in a dream of
and the moment when the illusion bursts
and stem and leaf stunned by the hand that
destroys whose then is the little voice to cry
injustice of the light and ampersand of mercy
displayed on the darkening glass is night
to claim and demand everything back are
the pronouns of subterfuge and will but

naught in the system of shadow-play we
are all about in the inch after inch of days
unnumbered and disremembered a blank
written and rewritten over the invisible
maze of loosely folded lives the recall of
grammar and math the situation of sun
in its lambent wavering diagonal toward
blackness shouts from the drugstore and bike
passing everything phantoms with Names !
the idiot stage where words are learned to
convey more than sound a sense of nostalgia
and longing for a lost silence the interaction
of mask and vowel the once and former sign
given to those vanishing from the phenomena
of being and becoming the smallest thumb
the index finger the clump of grass the dew
intake of breath and dizzying echelons stars
that by day are nothing more than painted
dots seraphim and instruments of unheard
notes the eloquence of the poet in his afterlife
so much to listen and so little to understand

06-29-20

IN THE CAVE OF POLYPHEMUS

"Aetnaeos vidit Cyclopas Ulixes"
Aeneid, XI, 263

never should have disembarked by the volcano
earth's violent tremors felt all the way to *mexico*
shaking seas fever blisters in the clouds skies
evaporating in brilliant starch-white haze
telegram home MOM we're lost please
send drachmae quick et cetera the memories
at times lascivious of the twentieth century
with motorized flivvers flappers dancing
with their knees and new hair styles meant
to madden how much is gone now how little
remains visible in the quadrant of atmosphere
where planets collide and the movie director
with his prompts and luncheon gadgets what
the hell here we are looking for the actress
whose suppose to enchant turning us into pigs

and the ear filled with roaring of rock and
lava are we but pygmies in this cyclical myth
stuttering prayer wheels laundry tickets
illegible and moist palms trying to recall
which words apply to which situation poetry
aside the mechanical rotation of vowels and
the fragmented syntax aphasic and sibylline
hiss hiss of the oracle droning drunkenly
like a hive suspended dangerously high
and listen ! cliffs talking to surging surf
waves violet and asbestos and sundowns when
reptiles encounter their shadows in the eyes
of immolated statuary deities reckoning on a
night in the abandoned seaside motel with its
circulating ceiling art depicting mortal women
disguised as philosophers discoursing on reason
and the idea of reason and what about us
trapped in the cave of desires prepared to
blind the giant with a burning stake and
overcome by the reek of offal and vomit
how trice the dream appeared gorgeous and
seraphic the erotic paradise of adolescence
and helpless all we could do was watch the fade
and intransigent metaphor of life and breath
choosing lots as to who would go and who
stay in this footnote of a mind gone AWOL
with an ear to the radio expecting coded messages
secret advice about the exit from this island
and the oceans of spray and unmitigated fog
home wherever it could be a solitary stone
leaves in isolation an echo of grass night

06-30-20

MORTAL ALL TOO MORTAL

still alive staring at the white stucco wall
caressed by large looming tobacco leaves
afternoon sun late in life and weary
reflecting on the hellenistic angel who
appeared to the shepherds as a matter of
phonetic change in the hills two thousand
years back using a hoarse form of Greek
pronouncing these words from a papyrus
I am naked mother how can one hear
such words tenderness that tears the heart
a magus could not improve and angel
suddenly aloft and larger than ever for five
full minutes hovered shining a brightness
on the stucco wall going into a trance
and can hear the dancers' feet on drum-heads
in an archaic two-step and in a dark swoon
folded in upon the self listening to
crevices forming in rock through which
hours seep turning into years just as sand passing
through a narrow bottle-neck becomes *time* itself
to die alone to remember almost nothing of
what went before emerging like a sound
out of the grass of memory and becoming
a ghost the thing that cannot return to
summer and home and trees and shadows
lying there vacant a husk of mind staring
rush of fragmented photo-glyphs of the past
lawns and careers and functions and fusions
fugue of effort and denial trial and failure
children whose sudden blossoming is curtailed
by a night-swoop of fate stars taken from their
trajectories comet-haired streaks turned to dust
a hand held for the last time eyes pleading for the end
inexorable heat and the vision of angel large
commanding the hills speaking with a singular
voice made of brass and pity in a dialect
none can understand the imminence of echoes
derived from a circle of consonants clustered
behind the blackening sun and what is more
than error a way of life of having mistaken
repeatedly the way through the wood and

burning gold branches and praying on wheels
that have gone wildly detached from the car
how many deities have simply sat on the top step
smoking cigarette after cigarette and clapped
come sundown and the cold of intransigence
wrapping around the knees and for why !
++++++++++++++++++++++++++++++++
vacant moons voided stanzas abandoned rooms
asterisk of singularity the universe pitched
from its height into chaotic theories of being
one and one never become two the loss is greater
than the sum of its hemispheres and what is to
understand lying there—stucco and tobacco leaf
ancient and porous bed-rock of mind
shattered kaleidoscopic empires of light
repeated and inconstant *I am naked mother*

07-01-20

TROBAR CLUS

difficult of access the intellect of heaven
portals wide that august avenues take and
of love's ferment the dilated seasons
that fill the eyes of promise with surfeit
reason to doubt and translate anew ancient
schemes that rhyme with sleep's amber swath
down slope the hills no more governed by
gods whose distant bays yawn with unseen
waters the vast is a portion of mind undetected
the sinuous willowy greens embroidering
memory of that first attempt and hidden as
ever the nymphs of laughter the trees arching
that ache to dissemble voices and sorrowing
was earth beneath the frail metaphor the
chain of syllables gone lost in airy prayers
or altars fuming with incense rare the cupola
of some divine transgression wrought through
language and its aftermath do we then mortals
astray in the dense wood of grief and propound
dialect and misery the vowels attuned to rock
the sage interpretation of loss the archaic
overwhelmed by seas abandoned by the sun

whose blackened whorls investigate other
spaces climes of complex consonants and
chimes that sound the ear's solitary afternoon
with resonance and echo of fragmented stone
statues half-finished whose blind center
like a magnet draws from light its breath
how bright was once the play of skirt
the hair-piece of burnished ebony the fix
between the hours that love employs
before death and time have their say

07-02-20

ELEGY : CORONA VIRUS SUMMER

so swift they say is a summer gone
no heat returns no fast running water
no verger eclipsed by dense green moons
no love as tender as lilac spray and no
poetry certainly of revived heroes armor
clad in verse of ethereal vowels and spun
like honey from a deity's eye the swell
and beautiful nights of an eternal June
the restless words on the lips of statues
declarations from the heart and mountains
bright with distance the forever longing
lovelorn screens and porches fragrant
with newly washed hair of nymphs who
taught the dance to fireflies and myths
how far a reach those missing days and
hours intoxicated with discovery of hives
and nooks and hills beneath the western
view and names tossed like declensions
from a forgotten Latin book and flights
of bee and hummingbird and the brain's
ancient yearning for the soul's unencumbered
being itself winging aloft in glassy flight
from the body's fading embers into clouds
and heavens that only last a minute
so much that summer gone the legend
of a hand among the leaves writing its
sad destiny and talking in the gravel
lingering twilights and lanterns large

as planets in a disappearing sky *reveries*
that life is infinite but like moths drawn
to the flame will burn instantly as
scattered ash and wings of memory

07-03-20

POEMA HUMANO

as Circe becomes pig so mortals
in reverie stupefied change souls
intransigence of fallen tower walls
the section by section partition of
air into vowel and threnody a lash
interprets its strike by a consonant
meant to double its effect in clouds
derived from a god's fractured head
wearing down speech in marble
grinding the whet-stone against
the winds of if its next of kin
speaking as a communist from
his algerian grave and foam
as wild as bric-a-brac in a fish's
eye to steam ahead as progress
when all around is down ruined
crescent and immobility to heave
each foot has its tongue and
each knee the teeth of piety
tombstone vision of the ankle
halcyon waves of indignation
because the state is a rudder a
temple in several hemispheres
a portuguese abscess in the mouth
how can one expect to speak like that ?
comma and gravel and purulent
destiny the fix is in the hand
and the hand is nowhere in sight
plus is one more than two and red
is the greatest concept of heaven
so leave it at that cavern and ivy
on the island where Circe ruts
grain and texture of servitude
man against man

07-03-20

THE FOURTH OF NEVER

unholy the day vestiges of fallen heaven
angels darkened by despair ruminate
in automobile graveyards a twisted
wrought iron cross dangling from a cloud
rows of crows on telephone lines jibe
at the diminishing azure of the distances
imperial hair-do crowns the fading glories
movie divas pretending to be mythic nymphs
water sprites dryads oreads the climbers
of skies but only futility banks its barges
on the rot-green canals that intersect
history the fuming altars abandoned by
deities of tin and cardboard bearing
names impossible to decipher in a bedlam
of vowels and concatenations of sound
no ear can disentangle from the remoteness
where death multiplies its consonants using
metal and pre-fabricated Latin colors
dumped into latrines and sewers befouled
by pretenders to the throne mountebanks
jugglers comic-book drawings of heroes
junkies and senators both on a sprawl
of dialect and aphasia incomprehensibly
out of touch with the ideolect of divinity
this corruption of the sacred light of day
even as sun casts its hoary blazing mane
traversing increasingly blackened heavens
toward a west grown puny with fanaticism
and an appetite for pornography and fireworks
this is not the symbol of the republic
for which it stands but the bared knuckles
of the drunken pugilist who has mistaken
the fraying ropes for the heart's intimacy
nights on a pub-crawl with broken minds
thought of empire and the drowning vast
of the starry empyrean a longing lost
in the diseased foliage of these last days

07-04-20

IMAGE OF JOE PLAYING THE TUBA
IN THE HOLIDAY MARCHING BAND

savage stars plucked one by one from
the night of time the illustrious ones
forever meant to shine like unspoken words
whose reverberating echo drills the sleep
of ears and hands burning in sounds and
phonemes of incomplete acts the mythic
innumerable causes inexplicable skies
ancient as yesterday's birthright and tomb
alive but once how can that be a brother
racing the grass for green and shadow
the leaves above and heaven in the roots
of trees that winter in the despond of man
casting late entries on the road to nowhere
the foretold ends of things an inch away
look at them wrangle the budding thoughts
like Castor and Pollux and their *sister* too
a hundred million times refracted in wastes
of water and light the former sun a blackened
whorl the way memory works fractioned
in its unshaped hemispheres and voices
loud as flags in a tempest wind or seas
underneath our feet the roaring cicatrix
of the hours each the furious opposite
of the other and why am I here and you
so far away ? *wake up* I keep shouting
shaking your head toss pollen in the air
make alive with imaginary bees the atmospheres
pull from the curtained tops of clouds
the glitter and spangle of our reveries like
the maps we used to draw and clustered the
hues and hills of endless days that never were
a schoolyard fence a ball flung at Olympus
the muses Nine in their fierce apparel
such as it was the hour of life in its myriad
illusive mirror and sphere of dreams
iterated in syllables of glass and bright
a loss at last each vow torn from the tongue
of leaves fluttering the articles of mind
now nowhere the cosmic trace of playthings
we used to dare the heavens with lessons

of hypotenuse and crimson fireflies
far-flung into the archaic firmament
as remote from here as the time you died
still marching as you are in your parade
finery a brassy never ending echo

07-05-20

THE WORLD THIS UNCOMMON PLACE

is it the same old story car-theft and kidnapping
of the bride pitting Argive against Trojan
are the consequences lost in miasmic detail
corona suns spinning out of control the bleak
and isolation and fade of all living things
withering like echoes in the leaf as dark comes
around for *this* umpteenth time over cocktails
an assembly of locusts at the round table a
distance of sound roaring in temple ruins
the cave the hill the glade the forest primeval
is it the constantly repeated mistakes over
loss of beauty over missing fragrances and
blooms ethereal and instantaneous on the steps
and book-learning and vituperation of glories
the chanting that cannot be heard bell-ringing
and drum-pounding the foot that cannot be
found the shoe in its equator of grief the solemn
vow to pronounce correctly at least once the
deity's *unknown* name and the paraphernalia
and equipment by which men ignore each other
the war games and lawns of retribution holy
the awesome instant of dawn's refusal to learn
charging her glistening steeds into the empyrean
are ink and parchment the only medium and ears
erect to the absence of night and sleepers beware
the foundation of sand the morass of dreams this
world this concatenation of illusions and children
fever-blisters canker-sores the invention of the phone
the voice-over on x-ray paper and memory itself
hostage to the nymphs of unwashed hair hard by
the river bank where love tarries growing wild
with broken promise the light that used to shine
and the unmitigated fossil stamped like henna

on the palm of the Buddha's hand left-ward
leaning like a statue of tropic wind and vowels
that interchange with the souls of infants born
before their time it is this *alas!* of sacred oblivion
the criss-crossing of the diurnal fever without
syllables the irreverent circularity of the mind
going round and round the faint blue distant dot
caught between the solar consonants and death

07-06-20

"YET BUT FOR A SCANT SPACE DID HIS STRIVING ENDURE"

the recovery never happened
stop and go the few minutes precious
we call life a sprig of lilac spray
a short visit to the mortuary
some burning tissue and smoke
rising in lazy curlicues into the
great absence called heaven

here lies so-and-so ever dear
to our hearts who in his brief winnowing
found air too dense and light too dark
aloft he went all wing and bright
the last leaf trembling on the branch
a voice no more an echo even less

was a hieroglyph a tiny notch a
frail attempt at writing a dream
in mirror-script a sequence of dots
asterisks commas and in the end
a hiatus yet be filled

wayfarer if you stop to look
gaze no farther than this clump
of grass where dew mapped its course
and vanished at the sun's first rays
pick a small flower and hold it
close to your breast and move on
the road ahead remains unknown

07-07-20

VARIATION ON A VERSE OF CAVALCANTI

"Fatto di sè tal servente,
che mai non déi sperare altro che morte"
    Guido Cavalcanti

dark around the knees wrapped as they
buckled and like a cut poplar hit the ground
what everlasting dust the eyes filled and
sorrowed in his heart the lost days of light
however tenuous was the tarrying by the banks
of the river Simoís entrusted to him the nymph
nameless now in the descent to Hades echoed
sound of sheep meandering without their shepherd
and head-first plunged into the depths where
like a wraith Persephone in her white-swirls
ineffable in her presence and heard about
the ears the plaint and lament of mothers
from the world above the strains of harp
and oaten reed the distances refraining rock
and darkness alike that sealed forever more
regret and the passage back to the stairs
now only smoke the pungent release and stains
of blood over stone and grass and ever more remote
memory of the face to him promised as pledge
of love her servant to be what else to hope
but death

07-08-20

AGAINST THIS MAN WILL I MYSELF ARM ME

shower of missiles darkened the sky by midday
sun's great orb nowhere in sight did captain *Karna*
fainted to the floor in his chariot still shine red-eyed
like lotuses afloat in far south and angered by taunts
his jeweled mind aroused once more to hurl more
than epithets heron-feathered arrows at his adversary
all in perfect Sanskrit the lore of rishis and demons
alike each verse the jibe and transgression of poetic
value the heights like mountains torn apart by winds
mightier than seas rocks folded like paper and sheets
of water you know the rest the outcome blood rush
gashes of earth the sundered planet somewhere betwixt

atmospheres and the gorgeous *Apsaras* plucking like
flowers in the field corpses more beautiful than life
into their passing chariots wheels protected by
charms uttered thousands of epochs ago and slanted
light coruscating bedevilment of reflections and echoes
their arms shimmering and the lopped heads staring
back into the Dravidian glaze of the afterworld far
to the beyond of time each turn of the mind each new
thought rising from before and fierceness of battle-
cry lion herds as it were feuding among each other
frightened deer sped into the hinter and still they kept
coming the dueling clans brother against brother
did I recognize in this array of moving photos Arjuna
and his charioteer and arrows sped into the fray
bolts of flame cherished with names long forgotten
you will turn the page no more read not a single
line past the instant when the triple-world seized
by its backside is hurled by some atomic Brahma
the final gesture and mimicry of literature aghast
the gods multiplied in their inch of space become huge
paramount illusions you reach this point of today
ancient with plague the world ! how does the cognition
of so much heat the circularity of phalanx array
the horses the three thousand elephants with their
majestic mahouts still crowd the paragraph of illimitable
description four by four the syllables packed into
a single word ! for why do you back off pondering
the parade of ambulances which are the punctuation
of man's effort to erase himself from the surface of text
nonsense and verbiage the ages folded and wrapped into
a ball and knee and shoulder and collar bone shattered
I am there again and again trying to finish the sound
OM in its decibels of clarity and darkness resounding
their faces like pallid moons caught in the wheels
of inexorable destiny doors that open and shut
volumes of illegible scripts hieroglyph and jackal
mountebank and illegal king endless endless night

07-08-20

THE PHOTOGRAPH SHOWING US BROODING AT THE HEIGHT OF ADOLESCENT MELANCHOLY

battle scenes shifting panoply across the great
screen of fireflies and unmitigated sorrows
each day of life one day less the ferment and tide
of memory crossing corn field and tundra alike
until the cities that shine and the enormous
citadel painted red for a moment only
followed by the music meant to lull the Pasha
confusion between man and his shadow the echo
chamber where the recitation of mute vowels
proceeds as if in a court of law you recall
don't you how we sat posed and poised with cigarettes
brooding faces countenances full of an unknown future
speaking Mexican in our thoughts and the pyramid
rising from the morass of corpses that fill a mountain
Venus writhing in silken chains Montezuma politely
bound by his captors just rooms away from power
brooding in the slanted light of our afternoon
either classical effigies or adolescent cadavers
replete with decline and fall of existentialism
and the concourse of myth and crumbling
Latin verbatim honeysuckle and willow bent
to the invisible pool where the heroes of make-believe
crouch to drink of the waters of oblivion
you were first to go on the errant episode of mind
making sure there was beyond the *other*
still another poignant moment to be lived
in the false narrative of the cinema of a bridge
and the river beneath bearing our masks away
what you discovered was the alternate hemisphere
of space and time the continent subdivided by watch-straps
and blazing embers your voice the fluted echo
of a distance I would never be able to span
the two of us frozen in time in the summer
of painted rocks and gravel driveways
posed and poised with cigarettes

07-09-20

THE UNFINISHED NUMBER

question the world of numbers
what is *the* one and how does it equal
anything other than the vanishing parameters
of dew and childhood the distances
between man and his shadow come nightfall
as well as *the* two or *the* three monstrous
equivalents of rain and sorrow the way knees
buckle under *the* four and the nuisance
of *the* five on the rise behind the mountains
poetry comes into being pondering questions
of rock and stone and eyes fill with grass
vision is eliminated the minute higher numbers
manifest like Chinese tones in the drilled ear
of the one who sleeps under the western hills
is this a decimal point away from the fraction
it takes to measure the lapsed hemisphere
of time and to ask and to remain silent
as the cycles of convergence and subtraction
go round and round dazzling the mind
with artifacts of myth and circumstance
ciphers too absorb plenitudes of history
counting backwards from the Persian *hundred*
right up the place where the ankles of nymphs
wade in pools of speculative math
quotients of mind and intellect and idyll
of love that abound in intricately counted stanzas
strophes of death and abandon all too human
the grief that comes profoundly when the unit *six*
is shouted in the ineffable countdown to infinity
enunciation of *zero* when the horizon clears
and all of space begins to rise like a glacier
of deserted light on the upper right of the absurdly shaped
numeral *eight* for what else is loss about if not
the algebraic equation that draws from the well
the plangent source of cognition to be born
and in the next minute to disappear
when only half the numbers of eternity have been
conceived as moons of rotation and suffix
clear nights on the porch of youth !
firefly and devastation of sex !
the rest of the poem is a threnody

a lamentation between the shoulders
paradigm of leaves trembling on a spear-tip
innumerable as are the figures of smoke rising
from the crematoria of memory

07-10-20

LE POÈTE MAUDIT

> "*I' prego voi che di dolor parlate*"
>   Guido Cavalcanti

the poets the damned and otherwise
from the depths despised or contrary
what to say of them how to speak
of the guise and delays of mood and tone
the bards and tripled by the crossways
the hastened to excess with word and verse
the syllable of distress the oath of vowels
uttered in sleep of distant trance of months
crowned by reveries of loves the mouths
reddened or chaste the breath dissolved
in fiery trace lip and ember soul and thread
lengthened to imply life and sudden how
they scatter death's whip before and
plead the muse forswearing ancient lore
stone and rock abide and light the merest
gleam and stars sprinkled over night's canvas
dire the heart's rueful chance and to dare
the following line to pursue unto the death
does grief the stronger dwell and sorrow
unkempt before the darkened wood to go
alone at last among dread murmuring leaves
the poets the poet the *one* entangled tongue
to brood and reflect all that has past
the end alone the day of loss is come

07-11-20

APPEARED TO ME A FIGURE OF DEATH

"Amor apparve a me in figura morta"
Guido Cavalcanti to Dante Alighieri

three o'clock bell rings school's out
down the street a gabbling rush of deer
spotted pelts large soft brown eyes liquid
pools where daily crowns the distance
it takes to reach the drug store or library
books and pencils and bent compass *the*
articulation of wind surfacing granite
creating ages in an instant before all space
descends from mind's small attic and ahoy
fingers wetted raised to the grazing breezes
ears alert to a song no one has ever heard before
a figure mysteriously garbed in sky-blue apparel
manifests briefly before the great engraved portals
brassy myth of medicine and time and there
on the top step as if offering cigarettes to
angels invisible but for their massive unkempt hair
did we know to understand this was the very end ?
the next day would be no more than a lamp
flickering in the tiny tempest of seraphic wings
spotted deer ! which of you has taken my heart ?
down the trailing and senseless path where
no motor dares to tread the rolling dusts
powders and incense and eye-liner the window
of paradise itself lifted from its frame
through which we see ourselves looking back
through the nostalgia of the years
today does not exist ! to have *never* been !
and consciousness itself in the tolling carillon
five o'clock and no hour has passed since three
my heart has been in rapture engaged
with the beautiful specter of death
for centuries now ever since I passed
as a phantom in the dusky Tuscan hills

07-12-20

I HAVE FOUND A BOOK

I am continually inspired by the mystery
the ineffable the angelic the behind the curtain
the enigmatic and archaic the rock and the stone
that stand sideways on the road I cannot travel
inspired by the genius of sleep and by sand
and the wind that gives birth to sand
and the sleep that wakes in sand and the circle
and the gyre and the chimes that lack ears
inspired by the glimpse and the hair and
the ribbons that hold the moon captive
when it has disappeared from sight
inspired by night the uncountable and by stars
punctuation of the mind on summer nights
when weight has no value and space finally
comes to end by the screen door where fireflies
hold court on the dilemma of light and voices
tiny and intransigent of the grass and the footprint
and shadow-play on the lawn where we have lain
and inspired by the *other* who is never there
inspired by marble statues deep in thought
by casual references to water and depth
by incessant hammering inside the leaf
which is echo constant and non-existent
inspired I am by memory of who I never was
the pronoun and the steeple and the word
that keeps repeating just like the dead
who can't stop dying and who live in me
who can't stop living though I am surely dying
inspired by the silence that surrounds each vowel
the concatenation and vibration of the sky
the many skies the clouds that cannot stay the same
and rain which is the alphabet of illusions
inspired by the gods all thirty three thousand and thirty
who have evolved out of a single dark consonant
and who have no past and envy mortals
their capacity for death
and envy mortals
their capacity for death

07-13-20

ONCE UPON A TIME

"ite, deae virides, liquidos advertite vultus"
Statius, *Silvae*, I.5, 15

go *green goddesses* turn your faces hither
rampant silver and verdant waters stream
from your reveries to watch other suns
rotate this vitreous noontime sky and heroic
poems of distances and hills opaque with mist
dun the heavens with gorgeous melody harps
by your fingers plied and song that drills
the mind with serenities of cloud and grassy knolls
the famous and fuming et cetera of incense
and archaic panoply of flute and spear the dense
clouds that loom before human fate and thrill
the ancient threnodies to tragic stage effects
do cluster names beyond the range of sound and
utter echoes that seem to rise from your inky
pools and if ever nymphs were meant to gather
in their fluid embrace deaths one by one it is
this moment woven of trance and ferny underpath
whole worlds of dream that glide from springs
into rock and fragmented stone oracular sleep
that divides mortal thought from its traces
and expends the atmospheres with lunations
of haunting brilliance screened by fireflies
of nostalgia and longing and never more to
return the bodies of wraiths translucent in their
tour of the other earth desperate for memory
of the hour on the river bank when the goddesses
green and shimmering evoked with crystal vowels
the sum of all living joys the transparency of
love and its winged imps whose piercing darts
the heart impaled and swept in a single doubt
the breath and space of that curtailed hour
the diamond hard instant of make-believe
as if dark spores the planets had never been
and their horoscopes a mesh of failed images
a ruin of sirens and syllables in the passing air

07-14-20

LET NOT AFFECTION FOR THE POET
PASS FROM YOUR HEART

what other cities are there and what shores
and seas exhausted by the myth of time
awash the corpses of a single deity surrender
to the light what memory remains and
what of the stellar deer hunted by Orion
and the blindness that comes with pride
and the sum of all forms repeated in *one* vowel
seers lost in the tangled wood of mind
and staff of bone and gnarled ivy bound
patter through untrodden paths the renown
of voice recollecting the ink of heights
are we but lesser beings in crumbling dynasties
of thought economy and history written
and unwritten nightly by the hand that dreams
who provokes the shape to take on its weight
infinite and constantly changing the rebuke
of poets and nymphs gathered on a knot of stone
far flung in the course of rivers to return
to their unbound source drowned legends
puerperal fever of the goddess in her plight
to simply understand the nervous strictures
of mortal kind such as we in our nocturnal deaths
how is one to survive the waking and walk
forth immune to the diseases of eternity
the metaphysical consonant the rite of smoke
that ascends as a body of oblivion and fingers
of cloud and grass and a childhood entirely made
of painted air the swings and columbines
stained with morning dew ere noon comes
with its heat to overpower all sweet promise
do we then wend our way through mountain
and defiles of lunacy and intoxication singing
as if to drill the moon's porous skin a dream as
ever of the will to shift matter from its core
to elements of ether and fire the emblazoned
inch of space where speech takes place as
a means for men to reckon their duplicities
we are come to this mausoleum entrusted with
a scant refrain and valleys and hills dun with fear
alas the tropes bards wield to render bright

just once what all have failed to realize
bone and nerve the winding trellis of wind
violet and azure swept away by the beauty
of this mad instant turning from breath
to the marmoreal stillness of the tomb

07-15-20

THE UNFINISHED DESIGN

where do we stand if not in the line of fire
in the inconsequential nation-state tithed
by the last Roman Emperor known to man
if not outside the pale if not within the mountain
shadows plying instruments of doom germ and mite
blood springs of nightmare cloudy recollections
of an infancy mired in the myth of progress
overhauling the mind with attributes of machinery
dot dot dot and abracadabra of the next big thing
isolationism not solitude metaphor and plight
substantives without form and unholy vowels
scattered like gunshot across the misty occident
if not just below the hem-stitching of the ideal
worn and woven around the mind the plastered
Venus of the suburbs the dominant paradigm
of corporate values structure and invisibility
nonsense of the myth of language as the invaluable
distinction of the species that has crawled up
from the swamp into some sort of empyrean
scheduled and reset for destruction in the near
future consumed by wild Siberian blazes melt-down
of the arctic circles injury and cicatrix of earth
revolving senselessly in uncharted space a fist
at a time the mouth wide open gasping for air
fish and colloidal seas trilobite and fossil-rock
the lung and its limited capacities and fern-print
under foot and the hasp and knuckle swinging
the gates wide open that lead to the Underworld
Persephone in her outdated clogs and hair-pins
mirror image of the Wraith who started the war
where do we stand if not in the penultimate day
of time worshipping what cannot be pronounced
asleep at the famous wheel drugged by Zeus

into thinking we are greater than our sum and
partitioned into verses and stanzas mantras
repeated in the jabber emanating from silicon
thrup thrup thrup the mechanical belt snaps
oil and misery and jungles decimated in a second
stocks and bonds ! where is the consonant that
breaks the bank where is the finger lost in grass
the fortune-teller and her raving tongue ?
lesser buddhas driving small vehicles of alcohol
on expressways that lead into the dark wood
words ! syllabic patterns of the ineffable
where we stand shadows and hieroglyphs
transparencies depicting the *unfinished design*

07-16-20

75,600 NEW CASES BREAKING RECORD

turn askance the right path was never taken
a list of losses of days without memory a frame
disappearing mists the tension in the wire
hanging by a single thought before the void
wasn't that a dark period of hospitals and
transfusions the lung displaced and the artery
going the wrong direction if only we had known
but the same things would have transpired
a budding during sleep a greening never felt
did the book open up did the pages require
renumbering and the saddest thing the shadow
stuck on the wall never moving as bidden
a fortnight later and the emptiness the paper
flowers the wilted stems in their yellowing
water and the mirror's systemic breakdown
could not have recognized who that was
reflecting back from a period of rock and
fragmented myth a stylized nomenclature
unearthly syllables the mouth could no longer
articulate the vowels in their closed sabbatical
a foreign moment before the shaking gate
and to enter and not look back and freeze
in the darkening light the evanescent sun
a black spore in the small space behind hills
twilit in a despond of quarry and nail-file

section at a time the air was dismantled
voices from torn leaves seemed to cry out
for the distant persons they used to be
how could we console one another *how* ?

07-17-20

EPITAPH FROM THE GREEK ANTHOLOGY

is the music of the spheres nothing more
than circus fanfare and the Olympic gods
but painted mountebanks and jugglers
tossing planets on a flimsy Ouija board ?
and what of men's lives the fragile
fabric airborne thoughts wings torn
in mid flight the drones and wasps
the smokes that strangle and hairs
in wisps and braids the fancy of death
all around bruiting stellar jingles an end
as always to the day's illusive joys
who was the first and who was the last
to fall on the dizzy lawn's summer play ?
alas the shout of distant cries mourning
hills resigned to opaque twilight shadows
and the city of crystal and invisibility lost
a last hour and the sorrow that follows
grieving feet and hives and trees aching
to touch the heavens and leaves with speech
of mortals the dying at every moment
when a toy hits the ground or a kite flown
into the dazzling inch of bright disappears
gone the token and the eye gone the ear
turned to stone or the tongue in its web
of vowel and echo and what remembers
but the husks of rising moons and months
named for sheaves of corn and soils
and to bed the everlasting in warm folds
that heat engendered among insects
who rule the restless southern fields
far from the motor-whine of automobiles
bearing the wary mind from its pattern
to the citadel of forgotten oceans
appeal of the dead in their paper boat

skimming time's endless inky stream
scant murmur fingers of grass and light
spent on the porch dancing in the dark
the *you* and the eternal gossamer *other*
what torch of fireflies flickering loud
in the absence love creates becoming
a single consonant spinning in the void

07-18-20

TOMBSTONE ON VIA APPIA

white dust in spirals a single puff
who mourns this passage these lost
echoes of feet on *Via Appia* long
submerged in the miasmic past
of a hundred untold tales and talks
winsome longing in pale arbors
grapes ripening in the moment musk
and tart the acids that run unseen
unsweetened fruits the gods pluck
souls of mortals husks and pods
a risk to breathe and wake again
morning in the leaf and sun bright
passing into the black seed did we
ever reckon the script to go blank
vowel interred with vowel in oblique
summons to return whence the dark
and alight with transparent wings
subtle creatures sublime entities
that call back to the vales and dells
rivulets rushing argent underfoot
the trebled voice of Hecate night-spun
whose hoarse moon dyes distances
wayfarer ! the prodigal minute is
come the transition from space to
unaltered space the vast unheard
and sculpted word inscribed in stone
margins of sound buried in memory
quarry and myth of blind statues
their mute appeal to the god whose
bow and shaft are ever poised

to take one more child unawares
and leave bereft the world behind

07-19-20

THE UNFINISHED PHOTOGRAPH

when we were teens the twixt and taint
the stain and opprobrium of consciousness
to think to bury stars at noon the heights
a splendor of mown grasses and eyes caught
between the harrow and the highway
earth's dumb machinery immobilized
by some errant deity whose mind is a cigarette
did we then pose for the bleak sun of death
a summer that begged for eternity
and painted rocks and chips of glare
the monsoon of thoughts that took our minds
what photograph could keep this up
this snarl of broken pedigree and heat
or was it unspoken longing for the Muse
the girl or nymph who spoke only French and
dilated the pupils of those whom she ensnared
the us of you and me the pronouns left
to dry in the shattered vestibule and
books in distant rows with titles of spleen
and atrophy how smart that made us feel
bigger than life the rest is verdure of tragedy
a whim to move from statuary myth
to the entangled consonants of living accident
gods pronounced alive in the pyramid of despair
to last no longer than the dragonfly shimmering
above the river Lethe's unheard echo

07-19-20

OFFICE OF THE DEAD

"Di vil matera mi conven parlare"
   Guido Cavalcanti

[a tableau of Rochester MN ca. 1956]
insect ghosts dried corn husks broken hair parts
combs with half the teeth missing faded red ribbons
the word *November* furrows where forlorn goddesses
bury their shadows shimmering selves disappearing
in the archaic home-town air raucous cries hoarse
vowels torn from missing words Spanish lessons
using only the honorific and drills and spades and ice
poetry books left to idle in motor oil sessions with night
when hours lose their meaning a music of rafters
and isotopes and the section of sky removed by
a buzz saw because it was yellowing shifts and tones
strange but lingering guitar chords that alter the ear and
the highway it resumes and the markers and erased
mileage signs and the enormous globe of the harvest moon
the home-coming queen in her saddle of ruined ivory
football and woolen mufflers and desperation to find
the right address a few blocks to the south where
the dead in their remnant of memory accost
the diesel truck carrying refrigerated minds and
radios from Tennessee and Arkansas haunted bluffs spirit-
worlds of lakota and ojibway and the dial that
fuels verses about heart-ache and crazy arms
fixtures with stove top and anklets the surprise
of a new language that has no consonants only bone texts
survival kit for the next world a fiction of
libraries and autumn sunsets and nostalgia and walking
home alone after an argument with girl-friend
the end of everything even as tilting like fuses of
light and amber the early evening stars announce
the possibilities of life somewhere else
+ +
the first cigarette and pabst blue ribbon and rapid schemes
to surpass water in the event summer doesn't return
stopped dead in the tracks of graduation
emptiness of the future and names robbed of sense
forget it all ditched and trundled and spent the night
deep in the oracular dark attended by a wraith
white on white the pallor of beyond and wet glistening

risen from the pool of oblivion to embrace you
and hours later with hangover and cruelties of ash
you are ready to die never mind the doorways
the frost painted windows and the avuncular advice
you remain alone a whispered afterthought
like the lyric on the jukebox—*Repenting*

07-20-20

DANCING IN THE DARK

> *"I' vidi donne con la donna mia:*
> *non che neuna mai sembrasse donna,*
> *ma son che somigliavan la sua ombria."*
>   Guido Cavalcanti

yearning of angels in despair
flight of time the senseless circling
meandering through dark vales of memory
window after window of missing faces
what can be said of the categorical imperative ?
with regard to the book you left behind
to the pages without number scrapped
with the words that lacked usage and
etymology and when pronounced and asleep
or in the dance with the minotaur
had no meaning and were but a music
tintinnabulation of cloud and lightning
you took the long thread unraveling
the source of its thought and if the door
was ever reached could it be opened ?
such as it was a breath at a time
the whole of life passed in that narcotic glare
leaf and hue and the distances encompassed
by dusk and the disappearing western hills
come evening the repetitions of echo
star-flicker and the eye enraptured and silent
would the sun ever rise again ?
then there was that mysterious woman
draped in veils of darkening enigma
she troubled your mind's swift asterisk
holding to it her brief lamp
you never had a chance to look twice
she was gone in an instant leaving

only her shadow around which
other women painted with gravity
danced

07-21-20

THE INFERNAL ROUND

the deaths of parrots lions and slaves
themes of Latin poetry suffused with
thought nebulous as the vacancies
of sleep and intoxication so it comes
around hyped and over-dubbed the cinema
of memory the fusion and fiction of
seasons collapsed all four into one
a single afternoon smoking weed and
drinking dago red and canned laughter
of the gods one by one bituminous and sulfuric
fascicules of rhyme a series of test questions
designed to pass the course Lucretius of
a summer and the demons hidden in eaves
and gables above the elegant commons dining area
trumpeting their mad jazz even as life
comes to a close the brief intermezzo
the patterned Homeric lies the hand
lifted waving magic baton over the presumed
entrance to Hell next to the gas pump
where the winos sleep it off and a blues note
survives the harsh night wintering a solo
to accompany the laboratory death
to its inconclusive bunker behind the bleachers
where they used to play football until literature
of a sort took over and patched eye and
dog-eared volumes of modernism and a lecture
on the steps Socratic and fulminant
who will attend this wraith in his passage
through the underworld footnoted
and divided by three as it all slowly
becomes Japanese medieval a forest dense
with blanched fogs hallucinatory voices
and off color singing in the torn leaves
are we for the rest of our lives to mourn
this youth so suddenly interrupted

waiting on the turnpike to hitch
a ride to Pluto's forbidden city ?

07-22-20

EJERCICIOS ESPIRITUALES

perpetual insomnia of mountains !
transgression of childhood spent
between the sky's eyelids while
ocher and dun hills weave twilights
a dream a trance a figment of speech
oracular sight ! hagiographic ears of the deaf !
not since the false inception of time
between the light-switch and the lightning rod
and you and I still talking to our own phantoms
illusive androgynous and hospitalized
toy and receptacle of thought
a hundred different ways to pronounce
the last vowel of the alphabet
and yet hindered by success we stammer
on the edge of the second line of the poem

is there a comma inserted in the hair-line ?
are we walking backwards in parallel lives ?
who has separated the sea from its asterisk ?
each has a text in the drama of tongues
but none has the memory to utter a verse of it
it aches in the dolorous plinth of the heart
shards of red-glazed pottery and ant-heaps
earth is a lore of strange bric-a-brac
pulmonary organs of history rotating
so we never know front from back nor
whether it began in Minoan script only to end
by splitting the atom below the bleachers
how is one to travel across invisible labels ?

the second person has no plural only
the ambidextrous phoneme ! particularity
and indivisibility of the statue in question
left brooding on river sedge late afternoons
what is a pronoun to the blackening sun ?
hiatus and abortion of consonants
each like a hand with no backwards

levels of cognition glimmering lunacy
shouting at invisible walls and the Trojan
fuse the illimitable vocation of air !
no one has taken the space to return
before the spear pursued its own echo
miasma and doctrine of memory
when nymphs washed their hair in dew
when hills their distance denied

it was time of the great recognition
skull facing skull in the mirror of doubt
reduction of the valedictory speech
on the top rung of a ladder of fire
her eyes were like blown smoke !
ejercicios espirituales ! tape-deck
with a medicated voice going in circles
will there be another tomorrow after this
one has been buried ? hasp and crook
lingering fossils of water and stone
the righteous indignation of marble !

peace to the mind
peace to the dialect of time
peace to the child in the grass
peace to the conflagrations of rust
peace to the oval and the fix
peace to the adjusted insect
peace to the empyrean of absence !

07-24-20

Iván Argüelles is an innovative and widely published Mexican-American poet. He was raised in México DF, Los Angeles, and ultimately Rochester, Minnesota. He received a BA in Classics from University of Chicago, and a degree in Library Science from Vanderbilt. A professional librarian, he was employed by the New York Public Library and the Library at UC Berkeley. A prolific writer, he has published numerous poetry collections, foremost among them: *"That" Goddess*; *Madonna Septet*; *Comedy , Divine , The*; *FIAT LUX*; *Orphic Cantos*; *Fragments from a Gone World*; and most recently *HOIL*, and *Twilight Cantos*. He received the 1989 William Carlos Williams Award for *Looking for Mary Lou*. In 2010 he received an American Book Award for his collection *The Death of Stalin*. In 2013 he was given a Lifetime Achievement Award from the Before Columbus Foundation.

BLANK PAGE BOOKS

are dedicated to the memory of Royce M. Becker,
who designed Sagging Meniscus books from 2015–2020.

They are:

IVÁN ARGÜELLES
THE BLANK PAGE

JESI BENDER
KINDERKRANKENHAUS

MARVIN COHEN
BOOBOO ROI
THE HARD LIFE OF A STONE, AND OTHER THOUGHTS

GRAHAM GUEST
HENRY'S CHAPEL

JOSHUA KORNREICH
CAVANAUGH
SHAKES BEAR IN THE DARK

STEPHEN MOLES
YOUR DARK MEANING, MOUSE

M.J. NICHOLLS
CONDEMNED TO CYMRU

PAOLO PERGOLA
RESET

BARDSLEY ROSENBRIDGE
SORRY, I BROKE YOUR PROMISE

CHRISTOPHER CARTER SANDERSON
THE SUPPORT VERSES

www.ingramcontent.com/pod-product-compliance
Lightning Source LLC
Chambersburg PA
CBHW030105170426
43198CB00009B/498